Books by Bob Chieger

THE CUBBIES
Quotations on the Chicago Cubs   1987

INSIDE GOLF
Quotations on the Royal and Ancient Game   1985
(with Pat Sullivan)

WAS IT GOOD FOR YOU, TOO?
Quotations on Love and Sex   1983

VOICES OF BASEBALL:
Quotations on the Summer Game   1983

The Cubbies

The Cubbies

Quotations on the
Chicago Cubs

Bob Chieger

Introduction by Tom Dreesen

Atheneum   New York   1987

Library of Congress Cataloging-in-Publication Data

Chieger, Bob.
    The cubbies : quotations on the Chicago Cubs.

    Bibliography: p.
    Includes index.
    1. Chicago Cubs (Baseball team)—Quotations, maxims, etc.   I. Title.
GV875.C6C47 1987   796.357′64′0977311   85-48139
ISBN 0-689-11782-5

The Cubbies

Quotations on the
Chicago Cubs

Bob Chieger

Introduction by Tom Dreesen

Atheneum   New York   1987

Library of Congress Cataloging-in-Publication Data

Chieger, Bob.
    The cubbies : quotations on the Chicago Cubs.

    Bibliography: p.
    Includes index.
    1. Chicago Cubs (Baseball team)—Quotations,
maxims, etc.   I. Title.
GV875.C6C47   1987   796.357′64′0977311   85-48139
ISBN 0-689-11782-5

Published simultaneously in Canada by Collier Macmillan Canada, Inc.
Composition by Maryland Linotype Composition Co., Baltimore, Maryland
Manufactured by Fairfield Graphics, Fairfield, Pennsylvania
First Edition

Baseball season approaches. The weeds are about to reclaim the trellis of my life. For most fans, the saddest words of tongue or pen are, "Wait 'til next year." For us Cub fans, the saddest words are: "This is next year."

George Will

The Pursuit of Happiness
and Other Sobering Thoughts, 1978

Contents

Preface

This book is dedicated first of all to Cub fans, past, present, and future, and to Cub players, management, and employees, who have made the wonderful journey with this team possible. In spite of the controversies, we can't forget that we still have Wrigley Field, the vines, a grass field, a true scoreboard, and day baseball. We have everything but a winner, but as every fan knows, everyone involved in baseball is a winner.

Special mention must be made of the sportswriters and other writers on the Cubs from whom I have quoted here. I hope that by my providing original sources and a complete bibliography the reader will be encouraged to seek out the complete texts. Some of the material was hard to locate, and I'd like to give special thanks to William L. Ohm, of Bill's Books in Stevens Point, Wisconsin, for providing us with rare books.

I'd also like to thank the Cubs organization, especially Robert Ibach and Ned Colletti of the Chicago Cubs and Bruce Bielenberg of the Iowa Cubs for their assistance, as well as Cub fans who are members of the Society of Baseball Research. Finally, I would like to thank the librarians and staff of the Chicago, San Francisco, Seattle, and Portland public libraries and the taxpayers who support these wonderful institutions. A book such as this would have been very difficult without them. It was made easier because of my editor, Ann Rittenberg, who deserves special mention.

Lastly, thanks to my father, Dan Chieger, who took me to ballgames as a young boy and who watched with the stoicism of a Gene Michael as his little shortstop, a possible Cub, let yet another go through his legs.

I hope the reader enjoys this book as much as I did putting it together.

Bob Chieger

March, 1987

The Cubbies

Introduction:
The Cub Mystique

by Tom Dreesen

My image of a Cub fan is of a middle-aged guy in the bleachers at Wrigley Field, in September, as he finally realizes the Cubs are out of it again. The game is over, the sun is going down, it's golden, and he's all alone, Wrigley is empty and quiet. All you can hear are his thoughts, the thoughts of every Cub fan. He's reflecting upon the team—and his life. He's thinking, "Gee, I remember when my dad brought me here, and he told me his dad brought him here, and then one day, I brought my son here. Those were great moments, but this was supposed to be the year. I was *sure* this was the year." His head is down, and as he walks out of the park, papers are blowing, the first tinge of autumn is stirring up. "I always thought the Cubs would make it to the World Series in my lifetime," he thinks. "If Sutcliffe had only stayed healthy, or if they could have whipped the Mets that first series." Then he turns for one last look at Wrigley Field, sighs, and says, "Wait till next year." Typical Cub fan. Sad and moving, but he reflects the hope that all of us humans have.

The last time the Cubs won the World Series, 1908, Teddy Roosevelt was president, and Ronald Reagan wasn't even born yet. Going back even further, on a day in 1876, the Cubs lost a game something like eleven to nothing, and at Little Bighorn, Custer was slaughtered. The paper was headlined "Cubs, Custer Lose Big." It puts it into perspective.

When the Cubs lost the National League Championship Series in 1984, I was in Los Angeles, and after they won the first two games in Chicago, I threw a party called, "It Was Worth the Thirty-Nine-Year-Wait Pep Rally." It was because if I still lived in Chicago, and our Cubs won the National

League pennant, it would be my instinct to go to the nearest tavern and celebrate. There were no corner taverns in L.A., there are no neighborhoods in L.A., to speak of, so I started a neighborhood tavern at The Improvisation. I went on the radio asking if there were any Cub fans to help me celebrate. I never knew it would be that big; we literally had to turn thousands away. One guy came totally painted in blue; he called himself a true-blue Cub fan. We were jubilant, and then, of course, things happened. We sensed the end when a ball got through Leon Durham's legs. We weren't worried even when Sutcliffe was struggling. Rick Sutcliffe was our messiah! He was sixteen-and-one that year with the Cubs. No. We knew Rick. Hey, no matter what you San Diego people do, Rick Sutcliffe is gonna come in here, and he's gonna win this last game, and we're gonna go to the World Series. Everybody knew that. Except the Padres.

Later on that year, I was on the *U.S.S. Norway* performing, and Rick was there vacationing. He's a good guy, a typical major leaguer of yesteryear; by that I mean you can have a few beers with him, he'll chew a little tobacco. He's just a regular guy. He tells a wonderful story about when he got mad at Dodgers manager Tommy Lasorda and went in and smashed the desk in his office. He picked up the desk and broke it in half while Lasorda cowered in the corner. Sutcliffe picked up a chair and was going to throw it against the wall when he looked and saw pictures of Frank Sinatra all over the wall. He said, "Aw, there ain't no sense getting Frank pissed off at me." And he put the chair down. Rick is a big fan of Sinatra.

When I was growing up in Chicago, I used to shine shoes in taverns from the time I was six until I was twelve. Sinatra was on every jukebox. I had eight brothers and sisters. We literally lived in a shack; we were what they call Shanty Irish. We had holes in our shoes as big around as an ashtray. We lived behind a factory. I had to bring money home to help feed the family, and my mother would take a nickel out and put it in a little cracked cup. Then she would surprise me with this money, and I would take the IC downtown and then the Elevated to Wrigley Field and sit in the bleachers and fantasize that maybe one day I'd be a bat boy. I finally got to be one thirty years later, when Cubs General Manager Dallas Green arranged it. It was that special year, 1984, and it was great; I got to meet a lot of good guys. Well, we lost the first three games of the four-game series, and I felt real bad. I went to manager Jim Frey and said, "Jimmy, if you don't want me to come tomorrow, I won't. Maybe I'm a jinx." He said, "Tom, if you stuck with the Cubs all those years we were losing, I guess we can stick with you one more day." Then they won, and since they knew I was feeling bad about the first three games, they all signed the game ball. Ryne Sandberg personally took it to each of the players. I don't care if I ever win an Emmy or an Oscar, because this ball is sitting on the mantel in my office.

You can talk about baseball's rivalries, but there is no greater rivalry in Chicago than the one between the Cubs and the White Sox. If they are both on television in a bar, arguments get so fierce half the people say they'll never come into the tavern again. In Chicago, the corner tavern is very, very important. The corner tavern is where you go to find out if Bob got the job, did Stella have the baby? It's a social center. Going there for the beer is secondary. Consequently, when a diehard Cub fan opened up a tavern, all other Cub fans knew that was the place to hang out. Same with Sox fans. But if you were really smart and wanted to open up a business, you tried to pretend you were neutral. I really don't know why they hate each other so much, I can't put my finger on it, but I know there are members of families who still don't talk to one another because one is a Cub fan and the other is a Sox fan.

There are more fans of the Cubs in the world than any other baseball team. The Chicago Cubs are truly America's team. The reason we love the Cubs is because the Cubs are survivors and so are we. It's because we identify with them. They don't win all the time, but they fight, and they try the best they can, and they oftentimes come up short. Most of us, like the Cubs, have some victories along the way, but not total victories. If you look over the life of a human being, 97 percent of this population will have some victories in their life, but they won't get that total victory, and that's the Cubs.

An analogy of the love for the Cubs could come from box-ing. You are sitting around watching a fight, a twelve-round fight. In the first round, the guy gets knocked down, and you say, "Oh, my God, is this guy awful." The third round, he's knocked down again. The fifth round, he's knocked down, and you say, "The guy's a bum, somebody get him out of there." All of a sudden, it's the twelfth round, and he's still there, this man is going out to fight three more minutes. He's had his ass kicked for eleven rounds, and you are saying to yourself, "Come on, you son of a bitch, please stay on your feet. Don't go down." THAT'S US. All we want to do is finish on our feet, and that's exactly what the Cubs are to us. They lose the total victory, but they finish on their feet. That's all we ask them to do for us.

Throughout our lives we struggle. There may be a death in the family that really sets you back; there's the loss of a job that you wanted so badly. A divorce. A woman leaves you. But you keep getting up, because somehow, in the back of your mind, you know that in your lifetime it will get better. And you know that about the Cubs. You know that somehow, before this life is over, the Cubs are going to win the World Series, and they are going to do that, JUST FOR YOU. JUST FOR YOU. You know in your heart, that when they win it, they'll be saying, "This is for you, Joe Stratovich, or you, Ethel Grimditch, this is what you waited for all your life, this is your personal victory." Every one of those fans is going to walk out of the ball park with that feeling: "They did it for me." So you can handle all the bad things that come your way in your life, because you know that before you die, the Cubs are going to win it, just for you. That's the way all Cub fans feel.

What exemplifies the attitude of the Cub fan is Ernie Banks. Twenty-six and a half games out of first place, and he walks out of the dugout, and he looks around Wrigley Field, and he says, "What a great day. Let's play two." Only a Cub fan could understand that. You see, today might be the day we turn this around.

I think that Cub fans probably have the fewest suicides of any fans in the world. See, we have something to live for. I worry that when the Cubs do win the World Series, you'll see a headline in the paper that says, "Cubs Win World Series: 20,000 Fans Commit Suicide. They've Been Wanting to Do it For Years, But Didn't Because They Had Something to Live For." But maybe they won't commit suicide right away because they have all winter long, all winter long to call their friends, especially the Sox fans, to call all those people who laughed at us. We have all winter long to write letters to all those people who teased us when we were young, who laughed at us in grade school because we were rooting for the Cubs, who ribbed us when we were in the service. Or maybe to call Uncle Al, who thought we were a jerk for rooting, and say, "Hey, what do you think about the Cubs now?"

When that day comes, there will be those friends and relatives who have passed away, who won't be there when the Cubs win. Though probably some guy sitting in the bleachers will be thinking to himself. "I sat here with my dad. My dad and my grandfather took me to Wrigley Field. Gee, wouldn't it be great if they were here now." But don't you understand? They WILL be there. You bet your ass, they are THERE. If you could do a movie on it, you would not only see a picture of all those Cubs who played in this ball park, you would see all those who ever came through those turnstiles with that same belief. On that day, when the Cubs win the World Series, they will all be there.

I used to wander aimlessly in odd jobs, and today I love my work. But I know I'm in the 5 percent. I know that 95 percent of the people in this world really do not know what they want out of life. They're wandering aimlessly; they don't have a goal that's SPECIFIC. But wanting the Cubs to win the World Series is SPECIFIC, that's something to hope for that's specific and clear. If nothing else is clear in your life, that's clear. There is no doubt about it: Unequivocally, you want the Cubs to win the World Series. And therein lies the hope. That hope people need to live their daily lives.

I think sometimes the players get a little jaded in their image of the Cub fan. Their image of the fan is this fat, loudmouthed, know-nothing baseball fan, but Cub players are lucky, because a lot of the Cub fans I've met are not that type. They are hard-working blue-collar workers, vice-presidents of banks as well as guys who sell newspapers on the corner. They know a little bit about the game, and they love the game as much or more than the players. Many of us are street guys, and we always dreamed we would lead the neighborhood through sports. We never thought about show business; we always wanted to know about the jocks. What kind of guy is Joe Namath? What about Mickey Mantle? They are our gladiators, because they are in the arena. When I go to the corner tavern back home, the guys say, "Hey, you're on Johnny Carson, that's great. You are opening for Frank Sinatra, that's terrific." But if you say you know Rick Sutcliffe, they'll say, "Hey, Tommy, what kind of guy is he? Is he one of us? Is he a regular guy?"

Baseball is like a play, there is skill, there's art, there's also the intensity of a guy like Pete Rose, and the great style of a Willie Mays. There's the gladiator and also the ballet dancer. But more important to me, I'm a street guy, and the most important pastime for us is hanging out. My wife used to think I'm out with other girls, but when she goes with me, she finds I'm hanging out. My best friends in Hollywood are all former street guys: Tony Danza—Brooklyn; Smokey Robinson—Detroit; Frankie Avalon—South Philadelphia; Boom Boom Mancini—Youngstown; and Frankie Valli—Newark. We don't go to dinner at Chasen's; we sit in the back of some joint and have a pizza and a beer.

The wonderful thing about a baseball game is we can go and hang out. They're changing innings, and they're changing pitchers, and there's time to bullshit, a time to tell stories, time to be with your friends. I love my wife and my kids, and I take them to the ball park once in a while, but there's NOTH-ING like going to the ball park with six or seven other guys. Back in the neighborhood—I must have done this 150 times —we used to have a bus pull up at the tavern, and fifty of us would go to Wrigley Field. We would hang out all the way down there, we would hang out at the ball park, we would hang out coming back, and guess what we would do when we got back? We'd go into the tavern and hang out some more.

We used to play softball four or five times a week; we'd play nine innings of ball on the field and thirty-five innings in the bar. Here's the joy of that. At the game, I'd say, "Good catch, Bobby." At the tavern, "Get Bobby a drink. Good catch out there in centerfield." Three beers later: "Bobby, some fucking catch out there." Midnight: "Bobby, in all my fucking years of playing that's the greatest fucking catch I ever saw." Last round: "Let me tell you something, Bobby, you know how many years I played this game, that was a catch. It saved our ass. Get Bobby another one."

Going back to the ball park, we can DO that at a ballpark. We can watch art, and we can hang out. Go watch a ballet and say to the guy next to you, "Hey, did I tell you?" And you'll hear all over the theater, "Shhhhhh. . . . !" Shhhhhhh? Give me the ball park any day. We can watch art and still bullshit. It's a love affair, going to the ball park. You know you're either going to come home joyful or sad, and what is love all about but joy and sadness? You're going to come home with feelings of friendship, kinship, joy, or sadness, all the things that belong in a love affair.

The Cubs were my first love, and maybe it's the greatest love affair of all. I have "Carolyn" tottooed on my arm. That's not my wife's name, that's my first love. She was my first love, and I'll never, ever forget her. You never forget your first love. When you are a little boy, the Cubs are your first love affair. Before you ever knew about little girls, you knew about the Cubs. Before you ever fell in love with a girl, you fell in love with the Cubs. I can almost picture a scene with a wife complaining about her husband going to Wrigley Field, and he's saying, "Look, I loved the Cubs before I ever loved you."

Bob Chieger and I spent some time hanging out, talking about the Cubs. We met in a strange way. About the same time I was writing him a letter praising his book, *Voices of Baseball*, he was writing his editor saying he wanted me to write the foreword to his new book, *The Cubbies*. Now that's magic between Cub fans. I was happy and proud to write the introduction. Bob has spent years putting together a book which comprises an oral history of this wonderful franchise, from its beginnings in 1876, when William A. Hulbert and Albert G. Spalding founded the Chicago White Stockings, soon to be called the Cubs, to the pennant years of 1906 to 1945, through the lean years, to the near-miracle of 1984, and back to the

hard times again. Any baseball fan will be enriched and en-
lightened by a reading of this book. Put it right next to your
Cubs cap, your Cubs jacket, your binoculars, your suntan oil,
all your equipment for the game. Share it with others. Soon
we'll write the final chapter of the story: the World Series.

We'll all be there.

*Tom Dreesen is a Chicago-born comedian who was the first
president of the Die-Hard Cubs Fan Club. He has appeared,
often with his Cubs hat, on over five hundred television
shows, and currently is the opening act for Frank Sinatra. He
lives with his wife and children in Los Angeles.*

1. Chicago

I'd rather be a lamppost in Chicago than a millionaire in any other city.
William A. Hulbert,
Chicago White Stockings president, 1876

First in violence, deepest in dirt, lawless, unlovely, ill-smelling, irreverent; an over-grown gawk of a—village, the "tough" among cities, a spectacle for the nation.
Lincoln Steffens
Shame of the Cities, 1903

A big city is not a little teacup to be seasoned by old ladies. It is in the big city where men must fight and think for themselves . . . the wilder the better for those who are strong enough to survive, and the future of Chicago will then be known.
Theodore Dreiser
The Titan, 1914

God, I can look the whole city of Chicago in the face and tell you I'm clean of the blood of every sinner, because I brought them their chance of salvation, and they wouldn't heed.
Billy Sunday, former Cubs outfielder,
at a Chicago crusade, 1918

Chicago is located just north of the U.S. I am well acquainted with the American Consul there. Chicago holds the record for murders and robberies and Republican Conventions.
Will Rogers
"Some Presidential Nominating Conventions," 1920

11

Chicago is justly known as the Windy City. Great winds come sweeping from the lake. And Chicagoans laugh, and say that they blow cobwebs from the brain.

Robert Shackleton
The Book of Chicago, 1920

Three of my friends were killed in the last two weeks in Chicago. That certainly is not conducive to peace of mind.

Al Capone, mobster, 1929

A real goddamn crazy place! Nobody's safe in the streets!

Lucky Luciano, mobster

At the Chicago gangster nightclubs they used to have an intermission—to give the audience a chance to reload.

Bob Hope, comic

In Chicago you feel the endless plains around you.

Simone de Beauvoir
America Day by Day, 1953

Chicago is an October sort of city even in spring.

Nelson Algren, writer

Most cities have a smell of their own. Chicago smells like it's not sure.

Alan King, comic

No one who wants to work in Chicago is unemployed. But it is a hard-knuckled city, a union town, friendly if one knows how to make friends, uptight to strangers.
Theodore H. White
The Making of a President: 1968, 1969

Chicago has survived and has maintained its incredibly rapid growth, in spite of fires, scandals, corruption and gang warfare. One feels an indomitable spirit there, an instinct for life.
Pearl S. Buck
America, 1971

Back to Chicago; it's never dull out there. You never know exactly what kind of terrible shit is going to come down on you in that town, but you can always count on *something*. Every time I go to Chicago I come away with scars.
Hunter S. Thompson
Fear and Loathing on the Campaign Trail '72, 1973

This is the mugging capital of the world. Why, I wouldn't go across the street at night in Chicago without taking a cab.
Harry Wendelstedt, umpire, 1974

What we do fear is riding the subways to get to the ballparks. Our local transportation network, the CTA (Catastrophes Twice Annually), has a safety record equivalent to that of the Three Stooges. They have accidents that cause traffic jams for hours, and I'm only talking about the ones in their yards.
Rick Schwab
Stuck on the Cubs, 1977

Chicago. A good truck driver took me through the core of the city, right through the Loop, and even in summer it seemed to me the bleakest, hardest, coldest town I've ever seen: I've never been back.

Edward Abbey
The Journey Home, 1977

There's a lot of violence there and it's easy to get sucked into it. I don't feel that way about New York, oddly enough. I feel that in Chicago I could very easily disappear—just drop out of sight—and nobody would ever know what happened.

Claes Oldenburg
The New Yorker, 1977

Claes Oldenburg showed his understanding of Chicago by producing a monumental replica of a baseball bat for a site on Madison Street, the city's north-south divider. Nothing, you see, divides Chicago like baseball.

Phil Hersh
Chicago Tribune, 1985

The city of "Where's mine?"

Mike Royko
Esquire, 1979

We don't have plastic politics here. The people of Chicago are very proud of their wickedness. This is good old vulgar politics, despite the pretensions.

Saul Bellow
New York Times Book Review, 1980

Chicago: Four ward heelers in rented tuxedos meeting in an opera-house lobby during an intermission of *Rigoletto* to discuss the rising price of embalming.

Russell Baker
New York Times, 1980

Chicago, a city of frontier spirit, where some say business is the highest art.

Maggie Paley
Quest/81, 1981

I put my suitcase down and I looked up at the Sears Tower and I said, "Chicago, I'm going to conquer you!" When I looked down my suitcase was gone.

James "Quick" Tillis, heavyweight fighter
San Francisco Examiner, 1981

Capitalism flows pristine and swift in Chicago, Illinois, the last place where a man can live and die over money.

Donald R. Katz
Esquire, 1981

We're very tolerant people. That's consistent with this Midwest, plodding way of life. The whole Second City syndrome. We don't mind being second. Obviously, if you look at the standings, we don't mind being fourth or fifth.

Kathleen Sheridan, Northwestern psychiatry professor
Inside Sports, 1982

For the Chicago fan, the Holy Grail is .500. There are no great expectations here. The goal is mediocrity.

Bill Gleason,
former *Chicago Sun-Times* columnist, 1982

There is no off-season in Chicago. It is only when the teams start playing that the fans lose interest.

Steve Daley, *Chicago Tribune* **columnist**
Sports Illustrated, 1982

Welcome to Chicago, where even the feast of Saint Valentine is associated with bloodshed. Chicago politics, like Chicago baseball, is not for the squeamish.

George Will
Newsweek, 1983

Real men don't eat quiche? Real Chicagoans won't even eat veal. Red meat rare, please. Big-shouldered, wheat-stacking Chicago fancies itself hairy-chested. But it has a baseball team, named for baby bears, that has been a byword for wimpishness.

George Will
Newsweek, 1984

2. Crosstown
and Other Rivals

I've already told [White Sox manager] Eddie Stanky that the North Side of Chicago belongs to me and me alone. If he dares to step into my territory, I'll have him tossed into the Chicago River wearing a new concrete kimono.

Leo Durocher, Cubs manager, 1966

I can't imagine it. It would be the biggest event since they closed the Coliseum in Rome.

**Jean Shepherd, humorist,
on a Cubs/White Sox World Series, 1976**

The only good thing about the White Sox is that a Sox game was the scene of my first sexual triumph. . . . On the way home, I managed to hold Jill's hand and was content knowing I had scored better than the Cubs.

Rick Schwab
Stuck on the Cubs, 1977

I was born and raised on the South Side of Chicago. . . . The Cubs were like people in a foreign country, as far as we were concerned.

Freddie Lindstrom, former Cubs infielder, 1979

They were Mayor Daley's team.

Barry Gifford, on the White Sox
The Neighborhood of Baseball, 1981

If a man tells you he's a fan of both the Sox and the Cubs, check your wallet, make sure your watch is still on your wrist, and lock your car doors. It doesn't work out that way in Chicago.

Jay Johnstone
Temporary Insanity, 1985

When I was a kid, I used to pray that the Cubs and White Sox would merge. It would settle all the differences and then Chicago would have only one bad team.

Tom Dreesen, comedian, 1985

I came out of it alive. By the time I was eight years old I was able to take a good punch.

Tom Dreesen, Cubs fan growing up in Sox country
Chicago Cubs Souvenir Program, 1986

Our fans don't want to be baseball fans or Sox fans. They are just Cub fans.

Dallas Green, Cubs president, 1985

The Cubs are quiche and white wine. The Sox are Polish sausage and draft beer. The Cubs are fern bars. The Sox are neighborhood taverns. The Cubs are power lunches. The Sox are heavy lunch pails. The Cubs are Ralph Lauren. The Sox are Oscar de la Rumpled. Cub fans are sopranos. Sox fans are basses.

Phil Hersh
Inside Sports, 1985

That's what I like best about Sox fans. They never whine. They might growl or bellow. And if they feel strongly about something, they might break your nose. But they don't whine. I guess it is their tough South Side heritage. I'm sure that 96 percent of all Chicago Yuppies, as well as 75 percent of the city's wimps, are North Siders.

Mike Royko
Chicago Tribune, 1985

I love the competition between the Cubs and the White Sox. But when they try to steal your organist it gets a little carried away.

Eddie Einhorn, White Sox president
Chicago Tribune, 1985

When I first met the owners, I didn't like them much and didn't trust them. Five years later, I like them less and distrust them more.

> **Harry Caray, on Sox owners Jerry Reinsdorf and Eddie Einhorn**
> *USA Today*, 1986

I can't tell you how many fans come up to me and say, "No matter what you do, beat the Cubs." I ask them, "Wouldn't you rather have us win the division?" You'd be surprised at how many say no.

> **Tony LaRussa, Sox manager, on the Crosstown Classic**
> *Chicago Tribune*, 1986

Atlanta Braves

Nothing in Atlanta is going to cause much excitement sports-wise unless it's drug-related. They are more concerned with Georgia peaches or football than they are about the Braves.

> **Gary Matthews**
> *They Call Me Sarge*, 1985

Fans out here say there are only two seasons, fall football and spring football.

> **Steve Stone**
> "Cubs Baseball," WGN-TV, Chicago, 1986

Cleveland Indians

My biggest problem in Cleveland was not pitching, because the Indians won seventy percent of the games I started. The rest of the time, it was hard for me to watch.

> **Rick Sutcliffe, Cubs pitcher, 1984**

I drove through Cleveland one day, but it was closed.
> **Jay Johnstone**
> "Game of the Week," NBC-TV

Cincinnati Reds

Did you know that in Cincinnati after two o'clock the only people you see are bartenders, ballplayers, and cab drivers?
> **Jim Brosnan**
> *Pennant Race*, 1962

Houston Astros

It's a twenty-five-million-dollar park with a nickel infield, a nickel outfield and a nickel scoreboard.
> **Leo Durocher, Cubs manager, 1969**

Los Angeles Dodgers

How about Dodger fans? It's more like, "Here I am at the game. Hi, how's my hair? Hi, how are you? Still working on that script? Oh, you did your nails today. Nice." I mean, they "dress" for games.
> **Jay Johnstone**
> *Temporary Insanity*, 1985

If there's a difference in fans out here compared with other cities, it's not the weather. It's the fact that fans here don't know what it's like to go through losing season after losing season. When you're the fan of a winner, it's like driving a Rolls Royce and never having to go to a garage.
> **Tom Bosley, actor and Cubs fan**
> *USA Today*, 1986

Minnesota Twins

Oh yeah, Minnesota likes water buffaloes—corner players who have power but can't run. And who don't have any bargaining leverage.

Brandy Davis, Cubs scout

Montreal Expos

It's a beautiful city, but much of the population is of French ancestry, and I'm prejudiced against the French. They eat snails. The women have skinny legs and the men have horse faces. The only times the French act pleasant are when they want us to rescue them from the Germans.

Mike Royko
Chicago Sun-Times, 1981

They discovered "boo" is pronounced the same in French as it is in English.

**Harry Caray, Cubs broadcaster,
after the Cubs swept the Expos**
The Sporting News, 1982

New York Mets

They say we're going to get players out of a grab bag. From what I see, it's going to be a garbage bag.

**Rogers Hornsby, former Cubs manager,
current Mets coach, 1962**

The umpires are cheating us because we're horseshit, and they know it.

**Richie Ashburn, former Cubs outfielder;
now a Met, 1963**

Unlike Mets fans, we can cheer a loser without becoming losers.

> **Jim Langford**
> *The Cub Fan's Guide to Life*, 1984

I wouldn't trade any one of our guys for any one of theirs—with one exception. I think we'd be able to find room for Dwight Gooden.

> **Rick Sutcliffe, Cubs pitcher, antagonizing the Mets**
> *Chicago Sun-Times*, 1985

I like our fans at Shea, but a few of them are the worst in the league. . . . Not even the infamous bozos at Wrigley Field in Chicago can match the New Yorkers.

> **Keith Hernandez**
> *If at First*, 1986

New York Yankees

A former New Yorker was babbling to me about how great his Yankees are, how they will win, blah, blah, blah, so I told him to shut his big, fat New York mouth. That made me feel good. If there is anything that can make me feel really good, it is hating the New York Yankees.

> **Mike Royko**
> *Chicago Sun-Times*, 1978

I didn't mind the pinstripes. It was the zookeeper who bothered me.

> **Jay Johnstone, former Cubs outfielder,**
> **on George Steinbrenner, 1985**

Philadelphia Phillies

No matter what I did in Philadelphia, it wasn't enough. You could hit two or three home runs in an inning, and if you made the last out, they'd still boo you.

Gary Matthews
They Call Me Sarge, 1985

Pittsburgh Pirates

He's really a Pittsburgh-type draft. Fast, black, a high-school kid.

Gordon Goldsberry, Cubs scout

St. Louis Cardinals

McCarthy, you don't have to worry about a runner on second base with this club. They just don't get that far.

Grover Cleveland Alexander, talking to his former Cubs manager Joe McCarthy, 1926

They've got too much energy. They knock you out of the way just for fun.

Jimmy Wilson, Cubs manager, on the baserunning of the Cardinals, 1942

They must have hit ten Baltimore Choppers, topped balls that bounced so high that Lou Brock, Garry Templeton, Jerry Mumphrey, and Tony Scott could get to Baltimore by the time they came down. The slower runners would only reach Indianapolis.

Rick Schwab
Stuck on the Cubs, 1977

They get to everything. But when they get there, they don't always catch it.

**Bill Madlock, former Cubs infielder,
on the outfield of Lonnie Smith,
Willie McGee, and George Hendrick, 1982**

I've watched the Cardinals on cable. When they get on base, it's like watching a pinball machine with lights going on and off.

Keith Moreland
Chicago Sun-Times, 1985

Champaign, it's the dividing line, you're midway between St. Louis and Chicago. A lot of cynical, opportunistic, weak-charactered people became Cardinal fans. The virtuous, serious Americans became Cub fans.

George Will, who grew up in Champaign
Chicago Cubs Souvenir Program, 1986

San Diego Padres

I'd played there in 1979, and, frankly, I thought the whole town was asleep or waiting for the next aircraft carrier.

Jay Johnstone
Temporary Insanity, 1985

San Francisco Giants

San Francisco, where a tavern brawl consists of two guys throwing fern leafs and clawing at each other's hairpieces.

Mike Royko
Chicago Tribune, 1986

Texas Rangers

This is a team going nowhere, which is easy to get to from Arlington, Texas.

Steve Daley
Chicago Tribune, 1985

Texas don't know baseball from barbecue.

Bernie Lincicome
Chicago Tribune, 1986

Mike Anderson   Phillies, Cardinals, Reds Outfielder
1971–1979

Decker: He must be battin' .411 against the Cubs. What kind of name is that, Mike Anderson. He sounds like he ought to be on "Father Knows Best." I bet that's not his real name.

Organic Theatre Company
Bleacher Bums, 1977

Sparky Anderson   Reds, Tigers Manager   1970–

Believe me, that is one smart man. He was smart enough to follow me to Cincinnati, and we went to the World Series. He was smart enough not to follow me to the Cleveland Indians or the Chicago Cubs.

Milt Wilcox, former Cubs pitcher, 1986

Steve Garvey   Dodgers, Padres Infielder   1969–

What you are hearing now is the reception for Steve Garvey. These fans are still wounded from the 1984 playoffs.

Bob Costas, on the boos at Wrigley Field
"Game of the Week," NBC-TV, 1986

Kirk Gibson   Tigers Outfielder   1979–

Gibson looks like Dick Butkus in spikes. He is a raw, bellicose, mustachioed moose of a hitter. During batting practice he is loud and profane and powerful, sending drives careening off innocent right field seats. Gibson, if he played in Chicago, would be mayor.

> **Bill Brashler**
> *Chicago Sun-Times*, 1985

Dwight Gooden   Mets Pitcher   1984–

When Dwight Gooden's on the mound, it gets late sooner than you think.

> **Herb Gould, after Gooden beat the Cubs**
> *Chicago Sun-Times*, 1985

Orel Hershiser   Dodgers Pitcher   1983–

On a day like this, you'd think we'd get ten runs. We couldn't even get anybody on base.

> **Jim Frey, Cubs manager, after Hershiser shut out**
> **the Cubs with the wind blowing out**
> **at Wrigley Field, 1985**

Howard Johnson   Tigers, Mets Infielder   1982–

We oughta send Howard Johnson a Christmas card.

> **Harry Caray, after he made six errors in the series**
> "Cubs Baseball," WGN-TV, Chicago, 1986

**Tony Perez   Reds, Expos, Red Sox, Phillies Infielder
1964–1984**

You should be ashamed of yourself, a fifty-two year old man
still hitting home runs. You should go and open up a restaurant.
**Don Zimmer, Cubs coach, after Perez
homered off the Cubs**
Chicago Tribune, 1985

Nolan Ryan   Mets, Angels, Astros Pitcher   1966–

The first time I faced my former teammate Nolan Ryan. . . . I
stepped out of the batter's box and looked at my bat. I was
looking for the hole in it.
Thad Bosley, Cubs outfielder, 1986

Mike Schmidt   Phillies Infielder   1972–

Schmidt never saw a Wrigley Field breeze he didn't like.
Bob Logan
So You Think You're a Die-Hard Cub Fan, 1985

**Tom Seaver   Mets, Reds, White Sox, Red Sox Pitcher
1967–**

He had a little better stuff than I did.
**Billy Connors, Cubs coach, on why Seaver is still
pitching fifteen years after Connors retired, 1985**

Darryl Strawberry   Mets Outfielder   1983–

Am I worried? How would you feel if you had to hold your
breath four times a day for the next two days?
**Jim Frey, Cubs manager,
on having to face Strawberry and the Mets, 1984**

3. The Cubbies: Over the Years

There were seven of us six feet high. . . . We wore silk stockings and the best uniforms money could get. We had 'em whipped before we even threw a ball. We had 'em scared to death.

King Kelly, White Stockings infielder,
on the team in 1882

Chicago should confine itself to the slaughter of hogs as a popular amusement because baseball seems to require more headwork than the city can muster.

***St. Louis Republican,* 1886**

Twenty-four, eighteen. There were twenty-four on one side of the grounds, and eighteen on the other. If he reports twenty-four *hundred* and eighteen, that's a matter of his conscience, not mine.

John Brown, White Stockings secretary,
telling a reporter of the forty-two
people in attendance, 1891

I suppose when I die, they'll put on my tombstone, "Here Lies Bonehead Merkle."

Fred Merkle, Giants infielder, who failed to touch second
against the Cubs, giving the Cubs the pennant over
the Giants and Pirates by one game in 1908

If he would only remember to run to second base when it is required—which reminds us of a man who had a thousand-dollar back and a ten-cent head.

New York Herald, 1908

If this game goes to Chicago by any trick or argument, you can take it from me that if we lose the pennant thereby, I will never play professional baseball again.

Christy Mathewson, Giants pitcher
New York Evening Mail, 1908

A one-legged man with a noodle is better than a bonehead.

Gym Bagley
New York Evening Mail, 1908

To tell the truth I shouldn't be surprised if we had a suicide or two right in this office. One of my deputies, I am sure, will commit suicide if the Cubs don't win.

Peter M. Hoffman, Chicago coroner
Chicago Tribune, 1908

The Cubs will be acknowledged as champions, but their title is tainted, and New York lovers of baseball will never acknowledge them as the true winners of the pennant. Whenever I mention the Giants from now on I shall accord them their rightful title, and I am firm in the opinion that I am right.

Sam Crane
New York Evening Journal, 1908

The game will never know another battle like that of 1908.

**John McGraw, former Giants manager,
shortly before his death in 1934**

They're all nice boys. Nicest bunch of kids you ever met. They faint at the sight of blood.

**Ed Burns, *Chicago Tribune* sportswriter,
on the Cubs in the 1930s**

Then in September we put on a real drive. We won twenty-one straight games. You ever go seventy-five miles an hour on the highway while everybody else is doing fifty? That's how we felt.

**Phil Cavarretta, former Cubs infielder,
on the 1935 Cubs**

If one system doesn't work, we'll try another. The trouble is that we're already on our third system.

Philip K. Wrigley, 1949

I always preferred Chicago rather than Chicago Cubs on the uniform. Cubs ends up on the stomach and that emphasizes it. Just Chicago across the chest makes them look huskier. Chicago Cubs looks like Joe's Garage.

Philip K. Wrigley

The 1947 to 1967 Cubs years were leaner than Cher. They never won a game they should have lost in that span.

Rick Schwab
Stuck on the Cubs, 1977

"I wouldn't know," Roy said. "I'm going to Chicago, where the Cubs are."
"Lions and tigers in the zoo?"
"No, the ballplayers."

Bernard Malamud
The Natural, 1952

Cavarretta should get a bonus for watching the Cubs every day this season.

Warren Brown, Chicago sportswriter,
on Phil Cavarretta's last year with the Cubs, 1953

You cannot think that I enjoy being harassed, ridiculed, and maligned for being president of a last place team.

Philip K. Wrigley, 1953

Look at this group. Looks like the Chicago Cubs outfield, circa 1953.

Joe Garagiola, to lounging media types
USA Today, 1984

The Chicago Cubs are like Rush Street—a lot of singles, but no action.

Joe Garagiola

It was the time of 3-D movies, Davy Crockett caps, Mickey Mouse ears, and the birth of rock 'n' roll. For the Cubs, the fabulous fifties were characterized by massive home run production but little else. The Cubs were the Edsels of the National League.

Eddie Gold and Art Ahrens
The New Era Cubs, 1985

Playing with the Cubs, you felt like everybody was waiting for the other team to win. In the late innings especially we'd figure out a way to lose somehow or other.

Dick Ellsworth, former Cubs pitcher

For the first half of the decade, the Cubs seldom rose high enough to swoon.

> **Jim Langford, on the 1960s**
> *The Cub Fan's Guide to Life*, 1984

If I can't win with one team, I'll back up the truck and get me another.

> **Leo Durocher, Cubs manager, 1966**

All Leo talks about is winning. He talks about it so much he gets you to thinking that the Cubs can be winners in '66. You have to wonder if he saw us play last year.

> **Dick Ellsworth, Cubs pitcher, 1966**

I never saw anything like it in my life. Our offense went down the toilet, the defense went down the drain, and I'm still looking for a pitching staff. I could have dressed nine broads up as ballplayers, and they would have beaten the Cubs.

> **Leo Durocher, on the collapse to the Mets, 1969**

The epitaph on the tomb of the 1969 Cubs reads: "Died from lack of leadership."

> **Jim Enright**
> *Chicago Cubs*, 1975

Naturally, I'm disappointed the Cubs didn't win. By now, I'm used to disappointments.

> **Philip K. Wrigley, 1969**

It [1969] was a season to remember. It was a season to forget.

> **Jim Brosnan**
> *Ron Santo, 3B*, 1974

That was when I first began to suspect that mysterious forces were at work. If we had the best team, the best players, then logic would dictate that we would win. But we didn't. Instead, a clearly inferior team, the Mets, came along and beat us in 1969.

Mike Royko
Chicago Tribune, 1984

Our North Side nine is one of the few championship contenders in history that has managed to lose ground while the team it was chasing endured six straight defeats. The Cubs non-accomplished this extraordinary feat by losing eight straight.

Bill Gleason
Chicago Sun-Times, 1973

Have you heard about the Cubs being sold to a group of businessmen in the Philippines? . . . Yeah, they're gonna move the team to the Philippines and rename them the Manila Folders.

Rick Talley
Chicago Today, 1973

I've been unhappy over the team's performance in other years, but there's only one word to describe my feelings about this season, and that word is—disgust.

Philip K. Wrigley
Chicago Daily News, 1973

Break 'em up. Splinter 'em. Back up the truck and ship 'em out. . . . If something isn't done—right now, before another season starts—the Cubs could well be on the brink of another twenty-year voyage to the bottom of the earth.

Robert Markus
Chicago Tribune, 1973

When they said, "Back up the truck," I mean, they really put it in reverse.

Billy Williams, Cubs outfielder, 1974

Do not go gently into this season, Cub fans; rage, rage against the blasting of our hopes. Had I but world enough, and time, this slowness, Cubs, would be no crime. But I am almost half-way through my allowed three-score-and-ten and you, sirs, are overdue.

George Will
Washington Post, 1974

About the only thing the Cubs didn't lose in the second half of the season was a night game at home.

Jim Langford, on 1974
The Game Is Never Over, 1980

One thing about the Chicago Bears. When their season starts, it sure takes the heat off us Cubs.

Bill Madlock, Cubs infielder

This is not a team, it's a satire.

Jim Murray
Los Angeles Times

Mary: I'm from Chicago. I know Chicago, my friends, my home, the *Cubs!* Everything that means anything to me is in this town.
Girl: You haven't been to a Cubs game in your entire life.
Mary: Well, they never seem to be playing the nights I'm free.
"Mary Tyler Moore," CBS-TV, 1976

Unfortunately, pennants aren't won in May.

> **Herman Franks, Cubs manager,
> in first place, 1977**

Marvin: You keep bettin' with your heart, not your head. These guys are fold-up artists. Nobody ever went broke bettin' against the Cubs after the Fourth of July.

> **Organic Theatre Company**
> *Bleacher Bums,* 1977

I used to idolize the Chicago Cub players and would have given *anything* if I could have gone up in the locker room to fraternize with them. It's kind of silly, but maybe I bought the Padres just so I could go in the locker room and kick one in the fanny and pat one on the back.

> **Ray Kroc, Padres owner, 1977**

When the Cubs are away from home, it's like a respiratory case leaving his oxygen tent. The club is as insecure as an obese third grader on the first day at a new school.

> **Rick Schwab**
> *Stuck on the Cubs,* 1977

The Cubs have made losing an art.

> **John Schulian**
> *Chicago Sun-Times*

There were times when the Yankee groundskeepers were much finer athletes than the Cub players.

> **Mike Royko**
> *Chicago Sun-Times,* 1978

As a lifetime Cubs fan, I was used to players who, as the sportswriters say, "can do it all." In the case of the Cubs, "doing it all" means striking out, running the wrong way, falling down, dropping the ball.

Mike Royko

I've had it up to here. Some of the players are actually crazy.

Herman Franks, Cubs manager, 1979

Preston Gomez was recognized as a strict disciplinarian. He wanted to build a ballclub on tight pitching and solid defense. Above all, he stressed speed. He inherited a club so clumsy and slow afoot that most players tripped over the foul lines.

Eddie Gold and Art Ahrens, on the 1980 team
The New Era Cubs, 1985

Spoilers! The only thing that we're going to spoil, we've already spoiled. And that's our season.

Rick Reuschel, Cubs pitcher, 1980

One sportswriter even suggested that the Cubs move to Gary, Indiana, and the reader was left to decide whether that was an insult to the Cubs or to Gary.

Jim Langford
The Game Is Never Over, 1980

Wrigley Field was full of ghosts for me. In comparison to the present day Cubs, the ghosts were far more pleasing to watch.

Barry Gifford, on 1980
The Neighborhood of Baseball, 1981

The Tribune Company had snapped up the Cubs a few months earlier for a bargain-basement $23 million. . . . The basement was the right place for the new owners to find a club chock-full of liabilities, most of them wearing Cub uniforms.

Bob Logan
Cubs Win!, 1984

Owned by the *Chicago Tribune*, the Cubs are sports' answer to the typographical error. Even referring to the Cubs as a baseball team leaves you open for libel.

Art Spander
San Francisco Examiner, 1981

It is well-known around the league that if you keep the game close the Cubs will beat themselves in the late innings.

Dallas Green, new Cubs general manager, 1981

When I first got here, I called some of our ballplayers first-and-fifteenth guys. They just played the game and got paid. If they won, it was neat; if they lost, it was no big deal.

Dallas Green
Sport, 1985

You have fourteen guys who can't play Triple-A, the free-agent pickings are slim, and there's nothing in the minors. Good luck.

Jimmy Piersall, former Chicago broadcaster, to Dallas Green, 1981

As the Cubs enter the thirty-sixth year of their rebuilding effort, there is the possibility of a player strike. If the Cubs withhold their labor, will we be able to tell the difference?

George Will
Washington Post, 1981

In some cities, where they have good teams, I can see where the fans would be upset. But the Cubs striking is about as significant as the buggy-whip manufacturers going on strike. What difference does it make?

Mike Royko
Chicago Sun-Times, 1981

Bowie Kuhn has not exactly been hitting his weight in the leadership department. He is the Chicago Cubs of commissioners.

Jim Bouton
San Jose Mercury News, 1981

The announcer says, "Will the lady who lost her nine children at the ballpark please pick them up immediately. They are beating the Cubs, 10–0, in the seventh."

Tom Dreesen, comedian, 1981

Other teams won and made it look easy; the Cubs lost and made it look hard.

David Brinkley
"NBC Magazine," NBC-TV, 1981

Do you realize the last time the Cubs won a pennant was 1945? There is no member of the Cubs today who was *alive* when they *won*. And when I joined they were in the thirty-fifth year of a rebuilding program.

Joe Garagiola
"The John Davidson Show," CBS-TV, 1981

This is going to be a funny monologue tonight. Look, if the Cubs can win a game, anything can happen.

Johnny Carson
"The Tonight Show," NBC-TV, 1981

If I managed the Cubs, I'd be an alcoholic.
Whitey Herzog, Cardinals manager

The Phillies beat the Cubs today in a doubleheader. That puts another keg in the Cubs coffin.
Jerry Coleman, Padres broadcaster, 1981

For the home of the brave,
The land of the free—
And the doormat of the National League.
Steve Goodman
"A Dying Cub Fan's Last Request," 1981

Don't send anyone down, don't send anyone down.
Fans' Chant, Triple-A Iowa Cubs, 1981

I knew what I had here, and I didn't have crap.
Dallas Green, Cubs general manager
Inside Sports, 1982

I thought this new tradition was going to change all that. I heard how these new players, these "gamers," were going to change everything. Instead of curing the disease, they caught it.
Herman Franks, former Cubs general manager, 1982

Recently, . . . the Cubs have had two problems: They put too few runs on the scoreboard and the other guys put too many. So what is the new management improving? The scoreboard.
George Will
Washington Post, 1982

I just hope there are a lot of guys who aren't back here next year. You get tired of looking at garbage in your backyard.

Lee Elia, Cubs manager
Sports Illustrated, 1982

We have a good bench. The trouble is, the bench is on the field.

An anonymous Cub
San Francisco Examiner, 1982

The latest diet is better than the Pritikin Diet. You eat only when the Cubs win.

George Shearing, pianist
KTVN-Radio, Las Vegas, 1982

The Cubs won the World Series in consecutive years, no less. The bad news is that the years were 1907–08 and they haven't won a Series since. There are seventy-three-year-old Cub fans out there getting the tiniest bit impatient.

Vic Ziegel
Inside Sports, 1982

Just stay close to them till Thursday. These are the 1969 Cubs. They fade.

Steve Stone, Cubs broadcaster, at the Cubs fantasy camp
Time, 1983

I never really fit into the Cubs image of a player, although you might think that after all those years of losing, they might want to change their image.

Bill Madlock, former Cubs infielder
Sports Illustrated, 1983

Like in the days of the old Boston Braves, who had "Spahn, Sain, and pray for rain," the Cubs have a rotation of Ferguson Jenkins, Steve Trout, and figure it out.

Robert Markus
Chicago Tribune, 1983

Always finishing at the bottom of the pack, Wrigley's chewing gum boys were much like Doublemint or Beechnut—they'd start off with a rush, then go totally flat.

Edward Kiersh
Where Have You Gone, Vince DiMaggio?, 1983

Basically, getting your ass kicked takes some getting used to.

Keith Moreland, Cubs outfielder, 1983

There's nothing wrong with this team that more pitching, more fielding, and more hitting couldn't help.

Bill Buckner, Cubs first baseman

He undertook a task that would have given Hercules a hernia.

Ray Sons, on Dallas Green
Chicago Sun-Times, 1983

Don't move, or I'll blow so many holes in you you'll look like the Cubs infield.

"SCTV," NBC-TV, 1983

So the Cubs have not won a pennant in nearly forty years. Look at it this way: In terms of eternity that's not even a flyspeck.

Jack Brickhouse, former Cubs broadcaster, 1984

The trademark of the old Cubs was to have clean uniforms. The trademark in St. Louis was, "Get your uniform dirty first, then talk to me." That's the way this Cubs team looks to me.

Lou Brock
Chicago Tribune, 1984

It has been seventy-six years since the Cubs won the fall classic. There is no record that the victorious squad ever received the now-common congratulatory call from the President, but if they had, it would have been Teddy Roosevelt on the line.

Steve Fiffer
Chicago Magazine, 1984

If you share my belief that all things come together for good, then how can we not believe the success of the Cubs bodes well for our nation's heartland?

Ronald W. Reagan, 1984

The Cubs are William Jennings Bryan, a prairie uprising against highfalutin Eastern plutocrats wearing spats, the Mets and Phillies. "Arise ye prisoners of starvation!"—that is the Cubs anthem.

George Will
Newsweek, 1984

The North Side die-hards stole the show,
The land of Wrigley is in my soul,
C'mon Cubbies let the good times roll,
Roll all day long.

Henry Farag
"The Land of Wrigley," 1984
Performed by Stormy Weather

It was for Ernie and Billy and Fergie and Randy and Ron and Don and Glenn and Leo and the rest of the class of '69. You can come out now, gentlemen. The long civic nightmare is over. From this moment on, the definitive moment in latter-day Cub history will be not that great collapse but this great triumph.

> **Ron Rapoport, when the Cubs clinched the division**
> *Chicago Sun-Times,* 1984

The Cubs had set another typical Cub record: the first National League team to win the first two games of the playoffs and then lose the next three. Why did it have to be us? Why do we always get stuck with such embarrassing records?

> **Mike Royko**
> *Chicago Tribune,* 1984

San Diego—Today's word, boys and girls, is choke. Can you say choke? Can you spell it? Will you ever forget it? Can you say ground ball? Could you catch one if you were eight outs away from the World Series? Could you catch two?

> **Bernie Lincicome**
> *Chicago Tribune,* 1984

I think they're more endearing in defeat than in victory. I like their loser-like quality.

> **Studs Terkel**
> *USA Today,* 1984

Call it angst, call it voodoo, call it alchemy, call it what you will. The Cubbies are cursed. After succumbing to the Padres in the playoffs, they all walked around the clubhouse like shocked survivors of a plane crash.

> **Peter Pascarelli**
> *Sport,* 1985

Once there was me and forty-five people in the whole ballpark. The crowd was so intimate instead of the National Anthem, we sang "Feelings." Before the game, I asked the vendor for a hot dog, and he said, "I only got one, just take a bite."

> **Tom Dreesen, in performance**
> Caesars Palace, Las Vegas, 1985

The Chicago Cubs, like life itself, are a losing cause. That's why we have cemeteries, and Wrigley Field.

> **Mike Royko**
> *Esquire,* 1985

Uncle Max had no patience with the long-suffering laments of Chicago Cubs fans who bemoaned their team's lack of success. "Suffering?" he'd exclaim, his voice rising. "Whatta dey know from suffering, dese ingrates? At least dey still got a team! Our team was robbed off of us! How could ya even compare it?"

> **Jay Feldman**
> "Is There Life After the Brooklyn Dodgers?" 1986

EX-CUBS FACTOR

You have to have a certain dullness of mind and spirit to play here. I went through psychoanalysis, and that helped me deal with my Cubness.

> **Jim Brosnan, former Cubs pitcher**
> *San Francisco Chronicle,* 1981

When you play with the Cubs, it's like playing with heavy shoes on. I had to be de-Cubbed.

> **Pete LaCock, former Cubs infielder, 1981**

Had I believed for one minute that my Cubs had done me in, I can assure you I would have gotten rid of them immediately. And if we get to the World Series next year and lose, I *will* get rid of them.

George Steinbrenner, Yankees owner, on ex-Cubs
San Francisco Chronicle, 1982

There is no such thing as an ex-Cub fan!

Jim Langford
The Cub Fan's Guide to Life, 1984

Remember all those articles in past years about how one team or another wouldn't win because of their "Ex-Cub Factor," the number of former Cubs on the team? Well, one reason the Cubs won this season is that they have the fewest ex-Cubs in their lineup!

Barry Gifford, quoting friend Steve Fagin on 1984
The Neighborhood of Baseball, 1985

We lost the 1984 World Series because of the Ex-Cub Factor.

Jack McKeon, Padres general manager,
who fielded three ex-Cubs, 1985

It's freaky, but it figures. The Chicago Cubs . . . just can't leave baseball alone. Twelve times a division winner had more than four ex-Chicago Cubs on its roster. Eleven times they have lost.

Bill Plaschke
Seattle Post-Intelligencer, 1985

I feel sorry for Toronto's fans. We carried three ex-Cubs in 1982 and now we have just one. That should tell you how we feel about it.

Roland Hemond, White Sox general manager, on the Ex-Cub Factor, 1985

4. Spring

On opening day, the world is all future, no past.

Lou Boudreau, Cubs broadcaster, 1948

Some players who go to spring training know they have the club made. Others think they do. Half of those invited only hope to. They don't have a chance.

Jim Brosnan
The Long Season, 1960

People ask me what I do in winter when there's no baseball. I'll tell you what I do. I sit and stare out the window and wait for spring.

Rogers Hornsby, former Cub, 1962

Usually on opening day I wear all I own and everything I can borrow. One year we had a snowstorm. The opposing pitchers threw snowballs at each other.

Jack Brickhouse, Cubs broadcaster, 1969

The Cubs had better stay right here until they get this right.

Bob Uecker, Brewers broadcaster, after the Cubs lost two games by a score of 22–2

That's the true harbinger of spring, not crocuses or swallows returning to Capistrano, but the sound of a bat on the ball.

Bill Veeck
New Times, 1976

Spring training is bullshit. Two weeks is all the players need to get ready. It's the fans that need spring training. You gotta get 'em interested. Wake 'em up. Let 'em know that their season is coming, the good times are gonna roll.

Harry Caray
Playboy, 1976

I go through a bottle of Alka-Seltzer each year on opening day. I'm always nervous the only day I'm sure the Cubs are still in the pennant fight.

Rick Schwab
Stuck on the Cubs, 1977

Spring, earth's renewal, a season of hope for the rest of mankind, became for me an experience comparable to being slapped around the mouth with a damp carp. Summer was like being bashed across the bridge of the nose—ninety times. My youth was like a long rainy Monday in Bayonne, New Jersey.

George Will, on being a Cubs fan
The Pursuit of Happiness and Other Sobering Thoughts, 1978

Do they still play the blues in Chicago
When baseball season rolls around?
Steve Goodman
"A Dying Cub Fan's Last Request," 1981

It takes a kid two minutes to travel the three blocks from the minor league complex to the major league complex. But it takes them two days to find their way back.

Tony Garofalo, Cubs trainer,
in Arizona, 1984

I love that sound of bats cracking in the morning air.

Joe Cuniff, Chicago teacher, in Arizona
The New Yorker, 1985

I think we need spring training to balance Groundhog Day. With the groundhog telling us to expect six more weeks of winter, spring training tells us not to worry, that spring is right around the corner.

Susan Greendorfer, University of Illinois sociologist
USA Today, 1985

This makes my thirty-sixth spring training, and I've never seen a group in such good shape so early. What are you staring at? My gut? I'm monitoring everybody else's progress.

Don Zimmer, Cubs coach
Chicago Tribune, 1985

I can't even remember coming to spring training in better shape. And I owe it all to spending my first winter in Chicago. Shoveling snow.

Keith Moreland, Cubs outfielder
Chicago Tribune, 1985

A year ago [in spring training], we lost eleven straight games, and I kept telling people I had a plan. My plan this year is to not lose eleven straight games.

Jim Frey, Cubs manager
Chicago Tribune, 1985

I was wondering if I'd make the traveling squad north myself.

Jim Frey, on the 1984 spring Cubs
Sports Illustrated, 1985

Openers are always beautiful. They are like newborns. For one day, everything about the season is perfect. Everyone starts even—from dynasties to doormats. Every team takes its first step. A baseball season awakens like a child opening its eyes.

Ned Colletti
You Gotta Have Heart, 1985

HoHoKam is Wrigley Field South. These aren't just exhibition games here. They are revival meetings. . . . This is where Cubs fans come annually to purge their souls of last season's sins. They come to forget about last year. They've spent the winter waiting for next year.

Steve Kelley
Seattle Times, 1985

My father, although he used to teach logic, does not understand this: It is dreadful to win a spring-training game, because a team is only going to win so many games in a year and why waste one in Florida?

George Will
Washington Post, 1986

In the spring, when someone asks you about your team's chances, even when you're on a bad team and know you don't have a chance, you still say that you do. Ernie Banks did that for twenty years.

Bill Madlock, former Cub
The Sporting News, 1986

We're not interested in sending any of our players up in a balloon at the moment, but check with me in April, when I see how good our team is. I might change my mind.

> **Jim Frey, when a company suggested delivering some Cubs to a game in a hot-air balloon, 1986**

5. Exercise, Diet, and Injuries

My mother said to me, "Your arm will be better as soon as the baby is born." And that's exactly what happened.

> **Gabby Hartnett, Cubs catcher, on his 1929 arm injury when his wife was pregnant**

Naw, I've started games dizzier than this.

> **Rollie Hemsley, Cubs catcher, after he was beaned, and it was suggested he leave the game**

I figured you might as well work on my left arm because I didn't want to deprive you of a job.

> **Kirby Higbe, Cubs pitcher, when trainer Andy Lotshaw rubbed up the wrong arm, 1938**

That's easy, call a doctor.

> **Andy Lotshaw, when asked what he'd do if a player broke a leg**

Andy had his own special "Lotshaw's Liniment." Most times he'd just pour Coca-Cola in his liniment bottle and rub the players down with that. They never knew the difference.

Rogers Hornsby
My War with Baseball, 1962

I was in combat two and one-half years as a paratrooper. I made thirteen jumps out of an airplane and never got a scratch. Now I get busted up for two months just chasing a little white ball.

**Hal Jeffcoat, Cubs outfielder,
injured when diving for a ball, 1950**

At one time I wondered how the catcher could have ten fingers on one hand.

**Harry Rush, Cubs pitcher,
on his astigmatism, which was corrected**

Felt pretty good when I got up this morning. But I got over it.

**Smoky Burgess, Cubs catcher,
his usual response when asked how he felt**

Not too bad for a balding old man with one leg who can't see or hear.

**Bill Veeck, his standard response
when asked how he was feeling**

Sit down, Jerry. You're too hurt to *play*. Your knee's sore. You could walk up and down Rush Street last night, but you can't start the next day.

Cubs fan, to outfielder Jerry Martin, 1980

Every time I walk by a scale they holler at me, "Why don't you jump on?" I work out every day and run, but I can't walk by a can of beer and smell it without gaining a pound. I just can't go to bed hungry. I'll wake up in the morning with feathers in my mouth, having eaten the pillow.

Bill Caudill, former Cubs pitcher, 1983

Somebody told me I look like Lasorda. As of now I am on a diet.

Jim Frey, Cubs manager, 1984

Ma tells me to watch my weight. Then she stuffs me with ribs, chicken, and all the trimmings.

Leon Durham, Cubs first baseman, 1984

I still don't understand how you get a sweet roll in that bloody contraption.

Don Zimmer, Cubs coach, looking at a blender
Chicago Tribune, 1985

I've always been high profile simply because I'm 6 feet 5 inches and 250, 260, 270 pounds, depending on what time of year it is.

Dallas Green, Cubs president
Sport, 1985

I wouldn't recognize a potato chip if it walked into this room right now.

Jim Frey, Cubs manager, on a diet
Chicago Tribune, 1985

I'm exceedingly proud of my staff. We were vulnerable to several culinary indiscretions last season, which is a polite way of saying we were all fat. The doughnut industry, we kept in business.

Jim Frey, Cubs manager
Chicago Tribune, 1985

It will be all right. It just hit in a bad spot, right on my funny bone. Except it wasn't very funny.

Shawon Dunston, Cubs shortstop, hit on the elbow
Chicago Tribune, 1985

No more Nautilus machines, no more aerobics classes, no more working out in the garage. These guys have got to start taking worse care of themselves.

Steve Daley, on team injuries
Chicago Tribune, 1985

This has never happened to me before. It was a terrible thing. You learn a lot about people in that time; you learn a lot about yourself. I didn't like what I saw of them or me.

Billy Connors, Cubs pitching coach,
on losing all four starters and more to injuries, 1985

Even when I worked hockey, I never say anything like this.

Tony Garofalo, Cubs trainer, on the injuries
Chicago Sun-Times, 1985

The injuries make the Cubs look like Confederate wounded at the Atlanta railway station.

Joe Goddard
Chicago Sun-Times, 1985

I didn't hurt anyone, other than someone in the centerfield bleachers. . . . I'm healthy. Horsebleep but healthy.

Rick Sutcliffe, Cubs pitcher, returning from injuries
Chicago Sun-Times, 1985

As much stationary bike riding as we do, we should win the marathon bicycle race. You don't ride a bike from first to third base. You run.

Dallas Green, changing the Cubs exercise program
The Sporting News, 1985

Trainer: Who's the president of the United States?
Zimmer: I don't know, but I didn't know before I fell off the bicycle either.

Don Zimmer, Cubs coach, after he fell off
an exercise cycle in spring training, 1986

I called Brian Dayett in my office and told him that's not a very good way to make the team.

Jim Frey, after the Cubs outfielder
beaned the manager in spring training, 1986

A couple of times he threatened to change places with me. Jody said he had better stuff than I did.

Rick Sutcliffe, returning from food poisoning
Chicago Tribune, 1986

Rick was really sick. Either that, or he'll do anything to avoid picking up a tab.

Jody Davis, Cubs catcher
Chicago Tribune, 1986

You kid about staying in shape. I see a lot more guys dropping dead jogging than going to the neighborhood bar.

> **Harry Caray, to partner Steve Stone**
> "Cubs Baseball," WGN-TV, Chicago, 1986

Stone: It's not unusual for a pitcher on a hot day like this to lose ten pounds.
Caray: Why can't we lose it up here in the booth?

> **Steve Stone and Harry Caray**
> "Cubs Baseball," WGN-TV, Chicago, 1986

Some players ask for a king-size bed or a water bed when they check into a hotel. All I ask for is a room near the ice machine.

> **Bill Buckner, former Cub, on his chronic injuries**
> *Sports Illustrated*, 1986

I mean, you can worry about a lot of things in this business and I've been hearing about people getting hurt on wet fields for thirty-five years. But I don't remember too many people getting hurt.

> **Jim Frey, Cubs manager**
> *Chicago Tribune*, 1986

I think they gave me Gene Michael's uniform. The buttons were popping. You know me. Whether it's Chicago or New York, I'm fat.

> **Don Zimmer, former Cubs coach, going to the Yankees**
> *Chicago Tribune*, 1986

Manny's O.K. But we had to put his helmet on the disabled list.

> **Tony Garofalo, Cubs trainer, after Cubs infielder Manny Trillo was beaned, 1986**

6. Rookies and Veterans

They have smelled the roses when they were in full bloom.

Warren Brown, Chicago sportswriter

I ain't what I used to be, but who the hell is?

Dizzy Dean, Cubs pitcher, late in his career

This is one day of my life I'll never forget. It's a wonderful feeling to be an immortal.

Gabby Hartnett, former Cubs catcher,
at his Hall of Fame induction, 1955

For a rookie breaking into the big leagues, every game is played under a bright sun with the flags waving and the Star-Spangled Banner playing between innings. It's the Mardi Gras and the home-town carnival all wrapped into one.

Joe Garagiola
Baseball Is a Funny Game, 1960

Was I scared? Well, I should have had a rope to tie my knees together.

Rick Monday, future Cubs outfielder,
on his debut in 1966

This wasn't a day, it was a lifetime.

Ron Santo, former Cubs infielder,
on Ron Santo Day at Wrigley Field, 1971

In baseball a player knows just two things: today and yesterday. There's never a tomorrow in a player's career until it gets here. I guess maybe it's better that way.

Billy Williams, in his last year with the Cubs, 1974

Now I remember why I retired.

Glenn Beckert, at the Cubs fantasy camp
Time, 1983

My arm has never felt better, so that's no problem. When I have my uniform on, it thinks it's twenty-five.

Ferguson Jenkins, age thirty-nine
Wall Street Journal, 1983

You lose your quickness. And you hear whispers. Rumors. "He used to make that play." "He used to hit that pitch." Or maybe they don't say anything, but you can see it when they look at you. You can see it in their eyes.

Ernie Banks, on when to retire
Sports Illustrated, 1983

Cey and Bowa are old enough to be dead.

John Schulian, on the Cubs infielders
Chicago Sun-Times, 1983

A couple of years ago in spring training, somebody wrote that the left side of our infield was old enough to be dead. If that's the case, two years later, we must be twelve feet under and all bones.

Larry Bowa
Chicago Tribune, 1984

I'm going to win the Illinois lottery, buy a baseball team, and make myself the first baseman.

Jay Johnstone, Cubs outfielder, released before the National League Championship Series, 1984

The only Hall of Fame that interests me is the one upstairs.

Leo Durocher, former Cubs manager
Chicago Tribune, 1985

Degrading? No, not at all. Down there, all they had to do was play baseball. They're not worrying about how much team-mates are making or how to keep Uncle Sam from getting his share. It was simple, and very innocent.

Rick Reuschel, as a veteran in the minors
Sports Illustrated, 1985

You can tell it well with the older guys, when they don't have it anymore. They stand out there on the mound, the poor suckers, throwing the ball so hard the sweat stands out in beads and runs down their face, but the ball doesn't move like it should, and you know they're through.

Lew Burdette, former Cubs pitcher
Chicago Sun-Times, 1985

When I came in the clubhouse, I stopped and watched Harry Caray on the TV. I saw the field and I said, "Wow, I was just playing out there."

Shawon Dunston, Cubs shortstop, breaking in
Chicago Tribune, 1985

Truthfully, the boos hurt a little bit. . . . I really thought I couldn't play the game. I always thought that when the ball was pitched, you hit it, and if the ball was hit to you, you caught it. I couldn't do either one.

Shawon Dunston, having problems
The Sporting News, 1986

I spent twenty-five years with the Cardinals. I thought I'd get a gold watch. They gave me a pink slip.

Harry Caray, Cubs broadcaster
USA Today, 1986

I'm a lifetime .240 hitter, and how many of them are in the Hall of Fame?

Dave Kingman, former Cubs outfielder
The Sporting News, 1986

The playing conditions in the Mexican League weren't bad—except for the heat. That's like saying that the first voyage of the Titanic wasn't bad—except for the iceberg. It was so hot in Mexico in summer that the flies just quit flying.

Thad Bosley, Cubs outfielder, 1986

The real thrill in this game is to finish it.

Lou Brock, at the National Old-Timers Baseball Classic
Sports Illustrated, 1986

I've been called too old since I was thirty-two. Sooner or later, you guys are going to be right.

Ron Cey, Cubs infielder, age thirty-eight
Chicago Tribune, 1986

7. Money

As you become more acquainted with ballplayers as a class, you will not be quite so liberal in your loans to them.
Albert G. Spalding, White Stockings owner, 1883

There are two classes of people whose wealth is always exaggerated by the great public. They are actors and ballplayers.
King Kelly, former White Stockings infielder, 1888

King Kelly had but one enemy, that one being himself. . . . Money slipped through his fingers as water slips through the meshes of a fisherman's net.
Cap Anson, White Stockings manager

Baseball owes me nothing. If I need help I can go to the county welfare office.
Cap Anson, when fired as White Stockings manager, 1897

I was not able to understand how it could be right to pay an actor, or a singer, or an instrumentalist for entertaining the public, and wrong to pay a ballplayer for doing exactly the same thing in this way.
Albert G. Spalding
America's National Game, 1911

Baseball is too much a sport to be a business and too much a business to be a sport.
William Wrigley, Jr., Cubs owner

He's the reason we made good money.
>Gabby Hartnett, Cubs catcher, on Babe Ruth

Folks, that's a great motto—when you're playing for free.
>Burleigh Grimes, Cubs pitcher,
>on "Humble in victory, gracious in defeat"

Heck, I can live a whole winter down home for $50. I can't live a week up here for that.
>Lon Warneke, Cubs pitcher, on returning
>to Mount Ida, Arkansas, for the winter

I ain't a holdout. I just don't want to sign this contract the Cubs sent me, because the dough ain't big enough.
>Babe Herman, who usually held out
>in order to skip spring training, 1934

You made me a mistake and sent me the batboy's contract.
>Pat Malone, pitcher, to Branch Rickey
>when traded from the Cubs to the Cardinals, 1935

When they gave me the $200, it was a check. I had never seen a check before. I told them, "I don't want this. I want money."
>Chuck Connors, future Cub, when at eighteen
>he signed a Dodgers contract, 1939

Jees. They're going to give me fifty thousand smackers just fer *livin'*.
>Dizzy Dean, former Cubs pitcher,
>when he sold the film rights to his life, 1951

It's so they can only move their heads sideways to say "no" when you ask for a loan. Those collars won't let them nod yes.

Bill Veeck, on why bankers wear high, starched collars

Beer makes some people happy. Winning ballgames makes some people happy. Cashing checks makes me delirious with joy.

Jim Brosnan
Pennant Race, 1962

A ballplayer has to be kept sort of hungry. There's never been a boy from a rich society family who ever played big-league ball.

Rogers Hornsby
My War with Baseball, 1962

After the season I went home for a month and then back to Philly to talk contract with Mr. [Gerry] Nugent. My hotel and food cost me more while I was there negotiating than the raise I got.

Kirby Higbe, former Cubs pitcher
The High Hard One, 1967

We're still about two Cadillacs apart.

Ken Holtzman, Cubs pitcher, negotiating his contract, 1968

We were awed when Philip K. Wrigley kept the price of chewing gum at a nickel for some nay years. Then P.K. surpassed himself. The owner of the Chicago Cubs topped all previous business coups by getting Billy Williams' salary on a one-year contract for the coolie salary of $150,000.

David Condon
Chicago Tribune, 1973

No ballplayer is worth over $100,000 a year. Three years ago, I signed Billy Williams for $150,000. I asked him if he realized he was getting three times my salary as Wrigley Company chairman. Know what he said? "So what?"

Philip K. Wrigley, 1977

My father was never particularly interested in making money. And neither am I. He always said that if you do the right thing, and build your bridges strong, it will come automatically.

Philip K. Wrigley

You can't manage these players today. They know it all. If you try to give them some advice, they'll show you that $300,000 paycheck and tell you to shove it.

Leo Durocher, former Cubs manager

I seldom refused autograph-seekers, unless they were old enough to look like collection agents.

Joe Pepitone
Joe, You Coulda Made Us Proud, 1975

You can have money piled to the ceiling, but the size of your funeral is still going to depend on the weather.

Chuck Tanner, former Cubs outfielder
Detroit Free Press, 1978

What modern player needs a salary advance? The only guys who borrow money anymore are the sportswriters.

Ferguson Jenkins, former Cubs pitcher, 1985

I had to give up some things I didn't want to give up—basically, cash.

Bill Madlock, former Cub, on his new contract
Sports Illustrated, 1985

It's basically what we were looking for—a lot of security. Now when I have children I can put them through college.

Bill Caudill, former Cub, on his $9 million contract
Seattle Post-Intelligencer, 1985

Money can't buy you love, it can just buy you temporary sanity.

Gary Matthews
They Call Me Sarge, 1985

I've met all sorts of people who wouldn't give me the time of day. I never met anybody who wanted to sell it to me.

Bill Veeck, when he saw the temperature was sponsored
Chicago Tribune, 1985

By paying [for bleacher seats], I kept my right to complain.

Bill Veeck, quoted in his obituary
Newsweek, 1986

To pay Ron Cey $1.45 million for the brand of ball he now plays is to pay for a memory. Memories don't stop grounders down the third-base line.

Allen Barra and George Ignatin
Inside Sports, 1986

Bruce Sutter. Allowing for taxes and the rise in the cost of living, he's earning slightly more now than God was in 1926.
Allen Barra and George Ignatin
Inside Sports, 1986

Thad Bosley, who will have to wait the full five years for the Cooperstown vote, no matter how much outside pressure is applied, told the Chicago Cubs he would settle for $425,000 for now, and even more next year if he should ever happen to make the starting lineup.
Mike Downey
The Sporting News, 1986

Let's hope Dallas remedies the few glaring discrepancies [in salaries]. He should begin by giving Frazier away to anybody who would take him. Maybe George could be given to some Little League team, and Dallas could get a tax writeoff for a charitable donation.
Jerry D. Johnson
The Scoreboard News, 1986

I was so poor, my first contract was signed in dirt. My first Christmas present was shoelaces. We spelled poor with only one o, because we ate the other one. When I was growing up, my favorite food was ice.
Mel Hall, former Cubs outfielder
Sports Illustrated, 1986

8. Catchers

Jimmy Archer   1904–1917

Old-timers used to compare Archer's arm to everything but a laser beam, and only because lasers hadn't been invented yet.

William Curran
Mitts, 1985

Roger Bresnahan   "The Duke of Tralee"
Hall of Fame   1900, 1913–1915

Darn them pads. Who invented them fool things, anyway?

Roger Bresnahan, who invented shinguards

He was also credited with inventing shin guards and chest protectors. Another big deal. If you get hit with enough foul balls, eventually you'll invent some protection.

Marty Appel, sportswriter, 1974

Smoky Burgess   1949, 1951

Smoky's a .300 hitter, but a .400 talker.

Richie Ashburn, outfielder

Burgess doesn't need a glove. All he needs is a bat and a pitcher to throw to hit. He can hit anything that doesn't hit him.

Al Hirschberg
Sport, 1967

If you woke Burgess up in the middle of the night and told him to get up and pinch-hit, he would line the first pitch into centerfield for a single.

Roger Angell
The New Yorker, 1982

The older he got and the fatter he got, the better his hitting seemed to become, until at the age of thirty-eight, Smoky weighed close to three hundred pounds and was hitting over .320.

Brendan C. Boyd and Fred C. Harris
*The Great American Baseball Card Flipping,
Trading and Bubble Gum Book*, 1982

Chris Cannizzaro   1971

He calls for the curve ball too much. He don't hit it, and he don't think nobody else can.

Casey Stengel, on the catcher's deficiencies

Harry Chiti   1950–1952, 1955–1956

The most interesting thing about Chiti is that he was obtained for "a player to be named later." When that player was finally named, it turned out to be Harry Chiti. Thus he was returned in payment for himself. There is no other reason for his fame.

Leonard Shecter
Once Upon a Time, 1970

In the old days you could watch Harry Chiti run to first base in thirty-five seconds flat.

Mike Royko
Chicago Tribune, 1985

Jody Davis   1981–

Davis can only improve behind the plate. But the way he hits, who cares?

Nick Peters, *Oakland Tribune* sportswriter, 1984

About time. They were starting to call me a defensive catcher.

Jody Davis, beginning to hit in August, 1984

Barry Foote   1979–1981

Foote's a gutty ballplayer, but he kept telling me we should have two buses, one for the players and one for the press, because that's how the Phillies did it. I finally stopped him by asking, "Do you want to be a first-string catcher here and ride one bus or keep carrying Bob Boone's jockstrap and ride two buses with the Phillies?"

Herman Franks, former Cubs manager
Chicago Tribune, 1979

Joe Garagiola   1953–1954

I know I find myself a helluva lot better ballplayer since I quit playing.

Joe Garagiola
San Jose Mercury News, 1980

I went through life as "the player to be named later."

Joe Garagiola
"The John Davidson Show," CBS-TV, 1981

When you're hitting .210, you're the clubhouse lawyer. When your hitting .350, you're the team leader.

Joe Garagiola
"Game of the Week," NBC-TV, 1981

Gabby Hartnett   Hall of Fame   1922–1940

When Gabby was catching, there were two umpires back of the plate.

Charlie Grimm
Jolly Cholly's Story, 1968

Gabby was, in the language of Chicago, "an old-neighborhood guy," which means that he never forgot where he came from, that the friends from the neighborhood were given top billing above the celebrities who were so proud to say they knew him.

Bill Gleason, *Chicago Sports* editor

He loved people, and people loved him. Gabby was a big man because he had time for the little ones.

Ray Meyer, DePaul basketball coach

Most catchers are so ugly they don't have to wear a mask, but I have to wear one because I'm so good-looking.

Gabby Hartnett

Rollie Hemsley   1931–1932

He could catch drunk better than most guys could sober.

Bob Feller

If Bill Veeck had minded his own business, Hemsley might have set a record by being arrested in every borough in New York in one day.

> **Mike Royko, on Hemsley's arrests in**
> **Queens and Brooklyn**
> *Chicago Sun-Times*, 1981

One writer said that Rollie was living proof that bourbon may lend wings to the spirit but not to the heels.

> **William Curran, on Hemsley's speed**
> *Mitts*, 1985

Randy Hundley   "The Rebel"   1966–1973, 1976–1977

Having Hundley catch for you was like sitting down to a steak dinner with a steak knife. Without Hundley all you had was a fork.

> **Ferguson Jenkins, Cubs pitcher, 1970**

Steve Lake   1983–1986

I had just fallen asleep when—wham! I sat up wide awake. I dreamed Lee Smith hit me right between the eyes with one of his fastballs while my mask was off.

> **Steve Lake, on his nightmare**
> *Chicago Sun-Times*, 1985

When people hear about Lake and Trout as a battery, they think they can think of funny things.

> **Steve Trout, Cubs pitcher**
> *Chicago Tribune*, 1986

Rocky Marciano   Cubs Minor Leagues

I didn't raise my son to be a catcher.

> **Mrs. Marciano, when her son**
> **finally chose boxing over baseball**

I couldn't hit the curve, but nobody stole on me. I'd rifle that thing down to second, and they were out by ten feet. And they were afraid to come into the plate and bowl me over. I was 5-11, 184, just like it was when I fought. I'd put the tag on 'em so hard they wouldn't forget.

> **Rocky Marciano, former Heavyweight champion**

Clyde McCullough   1940–1943, 1946–1948, 1953–1956

His swing had a hitch bigger than a Volkswagen pulling a yacht.

> **Rick Schwab**
> *Stuck on the Cubs*, 1977

Clyde McCullough looked like a cross between your local Army recruiter and the village hangman. He had a battered nose, a bull neck, barrel chest, gray-squinting eyes, blond-grayish-balding hair, and a slingshot arm. . . . He was the type whose uniform had to be torn off but no one ever tried it.

> **Eddie Gold and Art Ahrens**
> *The New Era Cubs*, 1985

George Mitterwald "The Baron" 1974–1977

Announcer: Batting eighth and catching, number fifteen, George Mitterwald.
All: Yay!
Decker: We used to call him Shitterwald, now we call him Hitterwald!

> **Organic Theatre Company**
> *Bleacher Bums*, 1977

Babe Phelps "Blimp" 1933–1934

He wanted to give the lie to the hoary charge that catchers couldn't hit their own weight. It might have made him batting champion.

> **William Curran, on the 225-pounder**
> *Mitts*, 1985

Steve Swisher "Swish" 1974–1977

Steve Swisher was one of those "can't miss" prospects who rapidly evolved into a "can't hit" suspect. . . . Swisher was dispatched to Wichita where he pounded the pill for a .196 average in fifty-two games. He was now ready for the Cubs.

> **Eddie Gold and Art Ahrens**
> *The New Era Cubs*, 1985

Elvin Tappe "El" 1954–1958, 1960, 1962

Elvin Tappe came to the Cubs along with a publicity promotion that would have done justice to Samuel Goldwyn in his heyday. He and twin brother Melvin were going to lead the Cubs to the promised land. They didn't tell us that the promise was seventh place.

> **Rick Schwab**
> *Stuck on the Cubs*, 1977

9. Infielders

Cap Anson   "Pop"   Hall of Fame   1876–1897

As a fielder, Anson was only slightly more mobile than a lamp-post. He was shifted around in the lineup but generally played at first base, where he could do the least harm.

> **Glenn Dickey**
> *The History of National League Baseball*, 1979

Gene Baker   1953–1957

Banks to Baker to Addison Street.

> **Jack Brickhouse, Cubs broadcaster,**
> **on the wild-throwing second baseman, 1954**

Ernie Banks   "Mr. Cub"   Hall of Fame   1953–1971

Without Ernie Banks, the Cubs would finish in Albuquerque.

> **Jimmy Dykes, Reds manager, 1958**

Ernie Banks swings a bat the way Joe Louis used to punch: short and sweet.

> **Clyde McCullough, Cubs catcher**
> *Sport*, 1967

I'd like you to look up the meaning of the word loyalty. After you do that, never come to me again with talk about trading Ernie Banks.

> **Philip K. Wrigley, to a Cubs executive**

Know how I'd pitch to you? I'd throw the old necktie ball. You can't hit on your back.

Satchel Paige, Athletics pitcher, 1965

Ernie Banks is the only person who would have been happy to be here.

Oscar Gamble, on the Yankees under
George Steinbrenner
Sports Illustrated, 1982

I asked him what he thought when he went to the plate and the game was on the line. He said, "Lola Falana at the beach." I figured if one of the great hitters can relax in those situations, so can I.

Terry Kennedy, Padres catcher
The Sporting News, 1985

Ernie Banks and I went to a Bears game, and the first three times the Bears got the ball they fumbled. Ernie hollered, "That's okay, that's alright, we're gonna get the ball back." I said, "Ernie, if I die and go to hell, I hope you're there because you're going to say, 'That's all right. It's going to get comfortable in here!'"

Tom Dreesen, comedian, 1985

During my half-month stay with the Cubs in September, 1953, I met more white people than I had known in all my twenty-two years.

Ernie Banks
Mr. Cub, 1971

Awards mean a lot, but they don't say it all. The people in baseball mean more to me than any statistics.

Ernie Banks
Mr. Cub, 1971

Dick Bartell "Rowdy Richard" 1939

On December 6, 1939, the Cubs quietly shipped Bartell to the
Detroit Tigers. . . . It was the end of an error, err, era.
Eddie Gold and Art Ahrens
The Golden Era Cubs, 1985

Glenn Beckert 1965–1973

I was wondering what a .239 hitting infielder was doing up
here until I spotted Leo. Now I feel right at home.
**Glenn Beckert, accepting an award with Leo Durocher
at a Chicago baseball writers' dinner, 1966**

Steve Bilko 1954

He hit nothing but homers in the minors and nothing at all in
several tries in the majors.
Daniel Okrent and Stephen Lewine
The Ultimate Baseball Book, 1979

Zeke Bonura "Bananas" 1940

He was a zealous disciple of the Cap Anson's "lamppost
school" of first-base play. . . . As for ground balls, Zeke would
as eagerly grapple a king cobra as put his glove in the path of
a hot smash.
William Curran
Mitts, 1985

He was no intellectual giant, but he understood better than
anybody in all of baseball the rule that says you can't be
charged with an error if you don't touch the ball. And so he
assiduously avoided touching anything that looked difficult.
**Edward Bennett Williams, Orioles owner,
graduation address, University of Scranton, 1986**

Zeke Bonura was nicknamed "Bananas" for good reason. He *was* bananas.

> **Bruce Nash and Allan Zullo**
> *The Baseball Hall of Shame 2*, 1986

Larry Bowa   1982–1985

Shortstop Larry Bowa, the team cynic.

> **Wilfrid Sheed**
> *The Nation*, 1980

I can show you an old psychological profile on Larry Bowa, where his "guilt proneness" is rated above ninety and his "emotional control" is below ten.

> **Jack Pastore**
> **Phillies Assistant Scouting Director, 1981**

After a sub-.200 start, he vented frustration with a bat, destroying a dugout toilet and knocking out lights in the tunnel to the clubhouse. . . . "Those were some of his best swings all year," cracked a teammate.

> **Nick Peters, Oakland *Tribune* sportswriter, 1982**

There are people who question whether Bowa has the emotional control. . . . But this is a guy who gets to the park before the grounds crew, talks nothing but baseball, and wouldn't know what to do with himself in a world of suits and ties.

> **Jayson Stark**
> *Sport*, 1984

The guy drove me nuts because all he thought or talked about was baseball. . . . After the games we'd go for dinner, then go home and watch the White Sox on cable TV. We did this for about ten days, and finally I said, "Larry, have you ever heard of 'Hill Street Blues' or 'Magnum, P.I.'?"
Jay Johnstone
Temporary Insanity, 1985

Grumpy little coot that he is, Bowa can still play shortstop.
Tom Callahan
Time, 1985

When he was going good, he couldn't wait for you [media] guys to come in the locker room for some more of his bull. When things went bad for him, he hid . . . Larry Bowa style.
Don Zimmer, Cubs coach
Chicago Tribune, 1985

Larry Bowa . . . would be doing all of us a service—himself, too—if he exercised one of the two options available to him: (1) quit, or (2) keep his mouth shut.
Jerome Holtzman
Chicago Tribune, 1985

Larry Bowa acts like he knows all the answers before I do.
Jim Frey, Cubs manager, 1985

Hell, Bowa ought to make a great manager; he's already had at least ten years of experience.
Bill Conlin, when Bowa became the Las Vegas manager
The Sporting News, 1986

I could take being called a blankety-blank. That didn't bother me. But when he called me a "blinkety-blank," he was history.
**Pam Postema, Pacific Coast League umpire
after ejecting Bowa for the third time, 1986**

Bill Buckner   "Billy Buck"   1977–1984

The last guy to run as badly as Bill Buckner was Long John Silver.
Mark Heisler, sportswriter

I thought he was the All-American boy. . . . What I found out, after being around him for a while, is that he's nuts. He goes berserk if he goes through a game without getting a hit.
Herman Franks, former Cubs manager, 1979

It was a joke that Herman [Franks] managed the Cubs at all. Against managers like Chuck Tanner and Dick Williams we started every game two runs down. For three years, he tried to be buddy-buddy, a grandfather to us. Then all of a sudden he realized that all he was to us was a big, fat clown.
Bill Buckner, 1979

The way Buckner tells it, the whole world's always wrong, and he's always right. Say hello to Buckner. Give him a kiss for me.
**Lee Elia, former Cubs manager,
his parting shot to Buckner, 1982**

Buckner: I don't like Charlie and he doesn't like me.
Fox: Buckner's paranoid. Who does he think he is? Does he think his shit doesn't stink? He's not that good.
Charlie Fox, Cubs special assistant, 1984

Never cared much for him as a player, really. Singles hitter, seems like he complains a lot. He's kind of a poor man's Al Oliver.

Bill James
The Bill James Baseball Abstract, 1984

It [the National League East title] was for Bill Buckner, who gave the Cubs seven good years, but whose greatest contribution to the team was leaving it.

Ron Rapoport
Chicago Sun-Times, 1984

I hate this place. Wrigley Field is the worst setting there is to play baseball. The fans are great, but you can't imagine how difficult it is to maintain your batting average around .300 in a park with natural grass.

Bill Buckner, 1983

Dolf Camilli   1933–1934

Nobody knew how well Dolf could fight because, quite frankly, nobody had ever wanted to find out.

Leo Durocher
Nice Guys Finish Last, 1975

Phil Cavarretta   "Phillibuck"   1934–1954

Chicago only began to exist for me as a real place, and to matter in American history, when I became fearful (as a Dodger fan) of the bat of Phil Cavarretta, first baseman for the Chicago Cubs.

Philip Roth
"My Baseball Years," 1973

Ron Cey   "The Penguin"   1983–

He's the only guy I ever saw who can circle the bases with a quarter between his legs and not drop it.

A scout

We ain't buyin' no duck!

Frank Lane, Brewers general manager

The first time I looked at him, waddling around the bases, I thought, "Jeez, can this guy play?"

Tommy Lasorda, Dodgers manager
San Francisco Chronicle, 1981

The first scout who recommended Ron Cey must have had more guts than anybody in baseball.

George Young, New York football Giants scout
San Francisco Examiner, 1983

Cey plays Candlestick the way Judy Garland played Carnegie Hall.

Michael Martinez
San Jose Mercury News, 1983

Let's put it this way—pigeons have been roosting on him for two years.

Vin Scully, on Cey's range
Los Angeles Times, 1983

Early in the game this little, bowlegged, gimpy guy got up to the plate and I thought, Jesus, do they expect this guy to hit me? I threw him a slider inside. Boom! Double off the left field wall. I watched him slide into second base and thought to myself, holy shit, imagine if this guy had two legs. I'd really be in trouble.

Bill Lee
The Wrong Stuff, 1984

With that body, "The Penguin" can't look well-dressed.
Marty Noble, *Newsday* sportswriter, 1985

He's the worst. You can't call strikes on him. He's never out. He doesn't like anybody. He doesn't even like himself. He's bleeped off because he's short.
Steve Rippley, umpire
The Sporting News Baseball Yearbook, 1986

Chuck Connors   1951

When Connors was suffering through a batting slump, he was a difficult man to share a continent with.
Tommy Lasorda
The Artful Dodger, 1985

I could've waited another ten years for Hodges to slump.
Chuck Connors, when told with the Dodgers that he'd play when Gil Hodges slumped

Babe Dahlgren   1941–1942

His arms are too short. He makes easy plays look hard.
Joe McCarthy, Yankees manager, 1941

Ivan DeJesus   1977–1981

Melody: But he dropped it.
Marvin: That's your boy DeJesus. Easy play, and he blows it.
Organic Theatre Company
Bleacher Bums, 1977

That's the first time in my life I've ever missed a grounder because of the wind. As I went down for the ball, a bunch of dirt blew in my face.
Ivan DeJesus, playing at Candlestick Park
San Jose Mercury News, 1981

Ivan DeJesus replaced Bowa, but last year he suddenly developed allergy problems. Unfortunately, it was leather he was allergic to.
Bill Mazeroski's Baseball, 1985

Sammy Drake   1960–1961

A bright lively chap who sat on the bench for the Cubs in 1961. That was the year he did not get a single base hit.
Leonard Shecter
Once Upon a Time, 1970

Shawon Dunston   "Thunder Pup"   1985–

If this kid runs too fast for the watch, maybe you can time him with the gun.
**Ed Katalinas, Tigers, to a fellow scout
in the minor leagues, 1981**

I know why they drafted the guy ahead of [Dwight] Gooden
—he's got a better arm.

Whitey Herzog, Cardinals manager
Chicago Sun-Times, 1985

Let's be honest. . . . At the present rate of Dunston's high, wide
and not-so-handsome throws from short to first, Leon Durham
may be applying for hazardous duty pay by the All-Star break.

Steve Daley
Chicago Tribune, 1985

Reporter: What about that unbelievable play the kid made
the other day?
Sandberg: Which one?

Ryne Sandberg, Cubs second baseman
Chicago Tribune, 1986

Shortstop Shawon Dunston . . . at twenty-three, he makes a
goofy play for every great one.

Dan McGrath
San Francisco Chronicle, 1986

Leon Durham   "The Bull"   1981–

His name is Leon Durham, and don't forget it. If they don't
know that name in Chicago by August, [general manager]
Bob Kennedy and I will be out of work.

Joey Amalfitano, Cubs manager,
when asked about "Leo Dunham," 1981

Johnny Evers   "The Crab"   Hall of Fame   1902–1913

He'd have to talk to somebody, even the devil if he was close by.

> **A friend, quoted by Jim Enright**
> *Chicago Cubs*, 1975

Johnny was a nonstop chatterbox on the field, to the extent that both Chance and Tinker sometimes wished he was in the outfield.

> **Donald Honig**
> *Baseball's 10 Greatest Teams*, 1982

Johnny Evers . . . was a maniac on the field. You hear a lot about Cobb being like that, but Evers was even worse.

> **Bill Wambsganss, former infielder**
> *The Sporting News*, 1985

Jimmie Foxx   "Double X"   Hall of Fame   1942–1944

When Neil Armstrong first set foot on the moon, he and all the space scientists were puzzled by an unidentifiable white object. I knew immediately what it was. That was a home run hit off me in 1937 by Jimmie Foxx.

> **Lefty Gomez, former pitcher**

Jimmie Foxx wasn't scouted, he was trapped.

> **Lefty Gomez**

Even his sweat has muscles.

> **Arthur Daley**
> *Kings of the Home Run*, 1962

He once started a restaurant and showed up for the grand opening four days late.

Bill Veeck, White Sox owner
Chicago Sun-Times, 1981

Charlie Grimm "Jolly Cholly" 1925–1936

You and your damn banjo playing and singing. You finally did it: singing yourself all the way to Chicago. You play good, but that singing. I just can't stand it.

Barney Dreyfuss, Pirates president, upon trading Grimm to the Cubs, 1924

Richie Hebner 1984–1985

Hebner dresses faster than he runs to first.

Marty Noble, sportswriter, 1985

Billy Herman Hall of Fame 1931–1941

Good. Very good. Ground ball had to be trailing smoke to get by Billy.

William Curran
Mitts, 1985

Rogers Hornsby "Rajah" Hall of Fame 1929–1932

I'd rather get into a ring with Dempsey than argue with Hornsby.

Sam Breadon, Cardinals owner, sending Hornsby to the Giants, 1926

He was frank to the point of being cruel, and subtle as a belch.

Lee Allen, baseball historian

I guess I tried everything. I gave him my high, hard one on the outside, and he belted it for a homer. I gave him a change of pace, and he hit a triple. I curved him, and he got a double. I threw him chest high, and he singled. I threw him knee high, and he tripled again. The only safe thing is to roll the ball up to the plate.

Jake May, later a Cub teammate of Hornsby

Rogers Hornsby, whose love of baseball was so great that it's a shame he wasn't born in Abner Doubleday's time. He would have beaten Ab to inventing it.

Charlie Grimm
Jolly Cholly's Story, 1968

Hornsby, who fought with nearly everybody during his long career, was then with the Cubs. He hated Cub manager Charlie Grimm and Grimm returned the compliment.

Murray Polner
Branch Rickey, 1982

He was old royalty, he represented magic, a crusty nobility. Maybe that .400 batting average is as near to a coronation that a nation that overthrew its monarchy gets. It sets men apart forever.

Donald Honig
Baseball America, 1985

Cliff Johnson 1980

When will Cliff Johnson run out of teams?

Jerome Holtzman (only nineteen to go)
Chicago Tribune, 1985

Don Johnson "Pep" 1943–1948

Don Johnson was *our* Ryne Sandberg.

> **Lennie Merullo, former Cubs shortstop,
> on the 1945 Cubs second baseman**

Billy Jurges 1931–1938, 1946–1947

He fought hard for the dollar at the conference table, but he fought a lot harder on the field. A one-day headache, yes, but always a season-long pleasure to watch playing shortstop.

> **Philip K. Wrigley, Cubs owner, 1954**

King Kelly Hall of Fame 1880–1886

My mother and father would never look at me again if I could prove a traitor to the boys.

> **King Kelly, turning down a bribe
> to help break the players' union**

It depends on the length of the game.

> **King Kelly, when asked if he drank**

He was a victim to fast living and a warning to all ballplayers.

> **Cap Anson, on Kelly's death from pneumonia**

Pete LaCock 1972–1976

Later that season [1975] I gave up a grand-slam home run to Pete LaCock, of the Cubs, and that told me it was about time for me to get off the mound for good.

> **Bob Gibson, former Cardinals pitcher**
> *The New Yorker*, 1980

Tony LaRussa   1973

The toughest thing for me as a young manager is the fact that a lot of these guys saw me play. So it's hard for me to instruct them in anything, because they know how bad I was.

**Tony LaRussa, who batted once for Cubs,
and not much more for three other teams, 1981**

He spends more time on the field now than he did as a player.

**Don Baylor, Yankees outfielder,
on the White Sox manager**

Davey Lopes   1984–1986

When he first came up, you couldn't get him to open up. Now you can't get him to shut up.

Ron Cey, Cubs infielder
Sports Illustrated, 1985

He's not particularly pleasant off the field, either.

**Marty Noble, *Newsday* baseball writer
naming Lopes to his "All-Mean Team," 1985**

Ever since I've been in professional athletics, that's what I've wanted—honesty. It's very rare. Mostly, I've heard, "Lopes, you're great." When I walk away, that same guy says, "That guy is nothing."

Davey Lopes
The Sporting News, 1985

Bill Madlock   "Mad Dog"   1974–1976

Batting in Candlestick is like trying to hit a cotton ball wearing an overcoat.

Bill Madlock

We'll trade Madlock if another team is foolish enough to have him.

Philip K. Wrigley, Cubs owner, 1976

Getting Madlock is the greatest deal since we bought Long Island from the Indians.

Tommy Lasorda, Dodgers manager
Sports Illustrated, 1985

Rabbit Maranville   Hall of Fame   1925

He once staggered out of the team hotel and got in a fight with a cabbie. He lost. So he picked a fight with the next cabbie and lost. He fought three more of them, and they all beat the hell out of him. So I asked him what he was doing. He said, "I'm trying to find one I can whip."

Bill Veeck
Chicago Sun-Times, 1981

Maranville played until he was forty-two. Had he led a clean life, he would have probably lasted until he was forty-one.

Mike Royko
Chicago Sun-Times, 1981

If there was a Hall of Strange, he'd be there, too. He often was seen in public with a parrot or monkey on his shoulder. He kept live fish in his bathtub and rabbits in his hotel room.

Robbie Andreu
Fort Lauderdale News, 1985

Lennie Merullo   1941–1947

Q: Everyone used to laugh at the immortal Lennie Merullo because he made so many errors at shortstop. And they laughed at the way he hit. But in 1947, he led the Cubs in stolen bases. How many bases did he steal?
A: Four. They laughed at him for that, too.

> **Mike Royko**
> *Chicago Sun-Times*, 1983

Eddie Miksis   1951–1956

Every litter must have its runt, but my Cubs were almost all runts. . . . All they could say about the Cubs infielder Eddie Miksis was that in 1951 he was tenth in the league with stolen bases, with eleven.

> **George Will**
> *The Pursuit of Happiness*
> *and Other Sobering Thoughts*, 1978

Joe Pepitone   "Pepi"   1970–1973

A couple of months later, he was playing in Japan. The last I heard he wasn't happy there, either. The Japanese people were very inconsiderate. They insisted upon speaking Japanese.

> **Leo Durocher**
> *Nice Guys Finish Last*, 1975

His most significant accomplishment was to introduce the hair dryer to the clubhouse.

> **John Lindblom**
> *San Jose Mercury News*, 1981

Pepi always believed the rules were for other guys. No wonder he was a Chicago favorite.
> **Bob Logan**
> *So You Think You're a Die-Hard Cub Fan,* 1985

Fred Pfeffer   "Unser Fritz"   1883–1889, 1896–1897

The greatest second baseman of them all . . . What a man he was to make a return throw; why, he could lay on his stomach and throw a hundred yards.
> **King Kelly, Cubs infielder**

Paul Popovich   1964–1967, 1969–1973

Sit down, Paul. We ain't giving up yet.
> **Leo Durocher, as Popovich began**
> **to warm up with the Cubs losing, 9–2**

Ruth 714 . . . Aaron 705 . . . Popovich 13.
> **Rick Monday, Cubs outfielder,**
> **writing Popovich's homers on a blackboard, 1973**

Ryne Sandberg   "Kid Natural"   1982–

Here comes Baby Ruth.
> **Whitey Herzog, Cardinals manager**
> **after Sandberg went five-for-six, 1984**

He's a good player and a massive babe.
> **Candace Butler, age fourteen, 1984**

They say he made six errors in 1984, but I can't remember any of them.
> **Jim Frey, Cubs manager**
> *The Sporting News Baseball Yearbook,* 1985

If you can't get along with Sandberg, you can't get along with your wife.

Don Zimmer, Cubs coach
Chicago Tribune, 1985

I was actually named after a former Yankee pitcher, Ryne Duren. . . . My sister was the only one who lucked out by not being tagged with a player's name. I don't know of any players named Maryl.

Ryne Sandberg
Ryno!, 1985

Ron Santo 1960–1973

In his rookie year as a pro, Ron Santo threw so many baseballs over first and into the stands at San Antonio that the team's general manager, Marvin Milkes, declared he was going to sell those first-base box seats at a premium since the fans who sat there were pretty sure to get a free baseball during the game.

Jim Brosnan
Ron Santo, 3B, 1974

Q: Which Cub great holds the record for most dirt rubbed into his hands during a career?
A: The immortal Ron Santo. His hands got so dirty that he used to wash them *before* he went to the men's room.

Mike Royko
Chicago Sun-Times, 1983

Dear Jack Brickhouse: I have a parakeet 1½ years old. He watches your telecasts and every time Ron Santo is batting he says "strike three." Why he picks on poor Ron I'll never know.

Jack Brickhouse
Thanks For Listening, 1986

Hank Schenz   1946–1949

He would do anything—pitch batting practice, catch batting practice, even sweep out the dugout after a heavy rain. . . . As Bill Meyer said, "Schenz can do everything but play regular."

Joe Garagiola
Baseball Is a Funny Game, 1960

Ted Sizemore   1979

He spent more time apologizing than playing ball.

Herman Franks, former Cubs manager
Chicago Tribune, 1979

Roy Smalley   1948–1953

'Twas an easy play, that tremendous clout,
Terwilliger to Smalley—to the dugout.

Phil Georgeff, Chicago racetrack announcer

When Eddie Miksis replaced Terwilliger in 1951, the main verse was changed to "Miksis to Smalley to Addison Street."

Eddie Gold and Art Ahrens
The New Era Cubs, 1985

From Roy Smalley I learned the truth about the word "overdue." . . . Smalley retired after eleven seasons with a lifetime batting average of .227. He was still overdue.

George Will
*The Pursuit of Happiness
and Other Sobering Thoughts,* 1978

Roy Smalley, who led the league in the number of vendors struck by balls thrown toward first base.

> **Mike Royko**
> *Chicago Sun-Times*, 1983

Chris Speier 1985–1986

We should have won. But Gary [Carter] called for a fastball when everyone in the league knows Speier can't hit a fucking curveball.

> **Keith Hernandez, Mets first baseman,**
> **when Speier knocked in the run that beat the Mets, 1985**

Eddie Stanky "The Brat" 1943–1944

Stank's the nicest gentleman who ever drew breath, but when the bell rings, you're his mortal enemy.

> **Leo Durocher**
> *Nice Guys Finish Last*, 1975

Steve Swisher 1974–1977

He's seen a lot of action, all right, but he's seen it from the seat of his pants in the dugout.

> **Hank Greenwald, Giants broadcaster**

Tony Taylor 1958–1960

Q: In 1958, Cub rookie Tony Taylor crossed himself and said a prayer every time he came to bat. What did this devout lad hit that year?
A: With the help of prayers, he hit .239 and slammed six home runs.

> **Mike Royko**
> *Chicago Sun-Times*, 1983

Manny Trillo "Indio" 1975–1978, 1985–

Acquired in a trade from Philadelphia [in 1982, to the Indians] Trillo turned out to be such a dog he couldn't pass a fireplug without lifting a leg.

Dan Couglin
Inside Sports, 1983

That Trillo makes nearly $200,000 more than Ryne Sandberg could be taken for evidence that God does not exist.

Allen Barra and George Ignatin
Inside Sports, 1986

Emil Verban 1948–1950

Undoubtedly the most remarkable aspect of Verban's career is his strikeout ratio. He fanned only 74 times in 2,911 trips. Heck, Dave Kingman can strike out 74 times in one month.

Eddie Gold and Art Ahrens
The New Era Cubs, 1985

Tom Veryzer 1983–1984
If he were a regular, he might be hurt so often that he'd never play.

Marty Noble, *Newsday* baseball writer, 1985

Billy Williams "Sweet Swinger" Hall of Fame 1959–1974

Hornsby: Suggest you bring up Williams. Best hitter on team.
Cub official: He's better than anyone else down there, huh?
Hornsby: He's better than anyone up there.

**Rogers Hornsby, Cubs coach,
at Triple-A Houston, 1960**

He is a serious, unemotional fellow who rarely opens a conversation. But he watches when a Mays or an Aaron or a Boyer steps into the batting cage, and *they* watch when Billy Williams takes his turn.

Mickey Herskowitz
Houston Post, 1964

I'm glad I didn't have to face him a fifth time. I ran out of pitches.

Steve Blass, Pirates pitcher,
after Williams hit two homers and two doubles, 1969

He might be guessing a lot at the plate, but he's sure guessed *right* a lot.

Randy Hundley, Cubs catcher

Williams comes from a long line of people who show up for work every day. Like all such, Billy was quiet, steady, dependable as a railroad watch. Every employer should have one. They give him a watch at the end of fifty years, and the boss' son, who inherited the business, notes at the banquet, "He never missed a day at the lathe in his life."

Jim Murray, after Williams appeared in
1,117 straight games
Los Angeles Times, 1970

The leader of the Cubs is, of all people, the quiet man of the clubhouse, Billy Williams. Billy Williams, who seldom speaks in a voice that can be heard beyond his own cubicle, who wouldn't say "Rah! Rah!" if Phil Wrigley promised him a $10,000 bonus for each "Rah."

Bill Gleason
Chicago Sun-Times, 1970

That guy Billy Williams is so good that even when he fans, a team is lucky to hold him to two bases.

> **Sparky Anderson, Reds manager, when Williams made second on a passed ball called third strike**

Sweet Billy Williams, quiet as an empty church, steady as the sunrise. Folks still looking for him, wondering why he hasn't been elected to the Hall of Fame yet.

> **Stan Hochman**
> *Baseball Digest*, 1985

Hack Wilson   "Sunny Boy"   Hall of Fame   1926–1931

Hack really hit fifty-seven [home runs in 1929]. He hit one up in the Crosley Field seats so hard that it bounced right back. The umpire figured it must have hit the screen. I was in the Reds' bullpen, and we didn't say a word.

> **Clyde Sukeforth, former Reds pitcher**

I batted behind Wilson. He cleaned the sacks and didn't leave any for me.

> **Hoss Stevenson, Cubs outfielder, when Wilson got 130 RBIs and Stevenson only 68 in 1940**

Wilson was a high ball hitter on the field, and off it.

> **Warren Brown, Chicago sportswriter**

Thus, he fashioned his famous life-style—ripping by day, nipping by night.

> **Jim Enright**
> *Chicago Cubs*, 1975

Hack Wilson usually played in the outfield, but I'd put him at first base because he wouldn't have as far to stagger to the dugout.

Mike Royko
Chicago Sun-Times, 1981

He jumped into the stands and beat up a fan. He said later he wasn't really mad at the fan, but he wanted to get arrested so he could take his hangover out of the hot sun.

Bill Veeck
Chicago Sun-Times, 1981

I've never played drunk. Hung over, yes, but never drunk.

Hack Wilson

Don Zimmer "The Gerbil" 1960–1961

I'm just a .235 hitter with a metal plate in his head.

Don Zimmer

Why he's beyond that. He's much more. He's the perdotious quotient of the qualificatilus. He's the lower intestine.

Casey Stengel, Mets manager,
when asked if Zimmer was the team's heart, 1962

By the time Don Zimmer got to the Mets all he had left was his hustle.

Leonard Shecter
Once Upon a Time, 1970

10. Outfielders

Richie Ashburn   "Whitey"   1960–1961

Either he throws the fastest ball I've ever seen, or I'm going blind.

Richie Ashburn, on Sandy Koufax

Frankie Baumholtz   1951–1955

The only Cubs outfielder to play left, right, and center at the same time in Wrigley Field.

Bob Logan, on the centerfielder who played between slow-footed Hank Sauer and Ralph Kiner
Chicago Tribune, 1986

Bobby Bonds   1981

When you're up there, it looks like you can hit him. Then it's like, "Here it is, . . . no it ain't."

Bobby Bonds, facing Fernando Valenzuela, 1981

Thad Bosley   1983–

There are people who think I play the piano better than I play baseball. Those are baseball fans, though, not music critics. Besides, Beethoven couldn't hit a fastball on the outside corner, either.

Thad Bosley, 1986

Lou Brock Hall of Fame 1961–1964

That is bush. Who are you trying to impress?
> **Dick Williams, Red Sox infielder, after young Brock**
> **slid headfirst in an exhibition game, 1963**

He's the only base stealer who can actually outrun the little white ball.
> **Jerry Koosman, Mets pitcher**

If and when he reaches the Hall of Fame in Cooperstown, New York, there should be a line on his plaque reading: *The Superstar the Cubs Had, and Let Slip Away.*
> **Jim Enright, *Chicago Today* sportswriter, 1976**

Don't be afraid to pull the ball next time, Lou.
> **Dennis Lamp, Cubs pitcher, after Brock**
> **drove hit number 3,000 off Lamp's pitching hand, 1979**

Brock . . . could get to the ball without difficulty. The question was what was he to do when he got there. . . . Only Reggie Jackson seemed for a time to have an outside chance of overtaking Brock. But he was rescued by the designated-hitter rule.
> **William Curran**
> *Mitts,* 1985

When I was a kid, I used to imagine animals running under my bed. I told my dad, and he solved the problem quickly. He cut the legs off the bed.
> **Lou Brock**

José Cardenal   1972-1977

Q: During spring training in 1974, a Cub star revealed that his eyelid was stuck shut and that this would prevent him from playing on opening day. Who was this strangely afflicted athlete?
A: It was the immortal José Cardenal. But his eye miraculously snapped open before game time when the fans sang "José can you see. . . ."

Mike Royko
Chicago Sun-Times, 1983

José denied the oft-told tale that he once missed an exhibition game because his eyelid was stuck, or another that a cricket chirped under his bed, keeping him awake.

Bob Logan
So You Think You're a Die-Hard Cub Fan, 1985

Even if José hadn't been a decent outfielder, he'd have been worth keeping on the roster just for his wonderfully imaginative excuses. José was the type who, if he couldn't give one hundred percent, thought it was best not to give any.

Bruce Nash and Allan Zullo
The Baseball Hall of Shame, 1985

Dominic Dallessandro   "Dim Dom"
1940-1944, 1946-1947

Little Dominic had tiny feet. It took him twenty jumps to get out of the dugout.

Mike Royko
Chicago Tribune, 1984

Bob Dernier "Deer" 1984–

If you were to watch him in some of the bigger parks, you'd really see some fine catches. At Wrigley Field, he runs out of grass pretty fast.

Jim Frey, Cubs manager
The Sporting News, 1985

Babe Herman 1933–1934

He did not run. He got to first base by sheer will power.
James T. Farrell
My Baseball Diary, 1957

Babe didn't worry much about his fielding. He wore a glove for only one reason: It was a league custom. The glove would last him a minimum of six years because it rarely made contact with a ball.

Fresco Thompson
Every Diamond Doesn't Sparkle, 1964

Floyd Caves Herman, known as Babe, did not always catch fly balls on the top of his head, but he could do it in a pinch. He never tripled into a triple play, but he once doubled into a double play, which is the next best thing.

John Lardner, Chicago sportswriter

Never once did I get hit on the head by a fly ball. Once or twice on the shoulder maybe, but never on the head.

Babe Herman

Babe did not always have his head in the game, especially when batted balls were on the loose. It was widely suspected that he was busy calculating his batting average through the last turn at bat.

William Curran
Mitts, 1985

Jim Hickman   1968–1973

These fellas ought to kiss his feet. Hickman carried us last year, and he's doing it again. We must be getting a little heavy for him.

Leo Durocher, Cubs manager, 1970

Hal Jeffcoat   1948–1955

Hal Jeffcoat was a strong-armed outfielder who threw like a pitcher. But, alas, he also hit like one.

Eddie Gold and Art Ahrens
The New Era Cubs, 1985

Jay Johnstone   "Moon Man"   1982–1984

Reporter: How did Johnstone end up in Oakland?
Rigney: Neil Armstrong brought him back from the moon.

Bill Rigney, A's executive

All winter long, you'd think this guy was Lou Gehrig. He was at every function. "Our guest today is the man who hit that pinch home run that helped the Dodgers win the World Series." The big dumb cocksucker got seventeen hits the whole year. Shit, Hooten had ten. Johnstone's the only guy who ever parlayed seventeen hits into a fortune.

Tommy Lasorda, Dodgers manager, 1981

Tommy Lasorda isn't really overweight—it's just that he isn't tall enough.

Jay Johnstone
San Jose Mercury News, 1981

He roomed with Piersall, hid from Danny Ozark, locked up Tom Lasorda, and dragged the infield with me. If there's anyone who is a product of his environment, it's Jay Johnstone.

Jerry Reuss, Dodgers pitcher

Don't blame me for Johnstone. He was crazy before I met him.

Jimmy Piersall, Chicago broadcaster

He wears Top-Siders, ties his sweater over his shoulders just so, never rejects an autograph seeker, is always fashionably late, scrawls personal notes, shaves with a chisel and a hammer, and would never, ever pick his nose.

Jay Johnstone, on Steve Garvey
Temporary Insanity, 1985

He gave me a chocolate hand by putting a brownie in my glove, then he gave me a stained head by putting chewing tobacco in my batting helmet. But what can I say? He's my friend.

Steve Garvey

Just once I'd like to slip up behind Johnstone and smash a cream pie in his face.

Al Campanis, Dodgers executive

The most amazing thing I've ever seen at Dodger Stadium was Jay Johnstone, in uniform, in line for a hot dog at one of our concession stands after the game had already started.

Fred Clair, Dodgers vice-president

He's missing so often he's the only player I've ever managed who needs a beeper.

> **Tommy Lasorda, Dodgers manager**

Here he is, alone with his thoughts. And Jay Johnstone? Only Jay Johnstone can know *his* thoughts.

> **Vin Scully**
> "National League Championship Series," NBC-TV, 1985

I'll tell you how Jay Johnstone got his nickname. One day he lost a ball in the sun, but when he came back to the bench he said, "I lost it in the moon." After that we called him "Moon Man."

> **Bob Rodgers, Expos manager, 1985**

About the best thing I could say about Johnstone is that he always thinks about other people. Whenever he forged my name on a dinner check, for example, he was always careful to leave a large tip so no one would think I was cheap.

> **Tommy Lasorda**
> *The Artful Dodger*, 1985

You mean to say I'm the only manager who never thought Johnstone was funny?

> **Jim Frey, Cubs manager, 1985**

Ralph Kiner   Hall of Fame   1953–1954

Ralph never robbed anyone else of a base hit, least of all a fellow slugger. I don't doubt that while there was still spring in his legs, Ralph ran after some things—taxis or blondes, perhaps, but never fly balls.

> **William Curran**
> *Mitts*, 1985

Dave Kingman   "Kong"   1978–1980

Just about anyone can be a sportswriter, I guess. If I can do it, anyone can do it.

> Dave Kingman, on his column in the
> *Chicago Tribune*, 1978

Hi, I'm Dave Dingdong, and you're not. . . . You might wonder why I've broken my legendary silence. Well, I'm a frank and honest person. And to be frank and honest, I'll do anything for a buck, even break my legendary silence. And if you wonder why I've been silent for so long, it's because basically I'm a shallow, self-centered person who has few ideas and nothing to say.

> Mike Royko, parodying Kingman's column
> *Chicago Sun-Times*, 1978

An empty paint can being thrown from a car at sixty miles per hour.

> John Schulian, on Kingman's dive for a ball
> *Chicago Sun-Times*

Unless someone can prove that Kingman got lost on the way home from nursery school one afternoon and wound up playing major league baseball, he has run out of acceptable excuses for his boorish, childish behavior.

> David Israel
> *Chicago Tribune*

He's misunderstood. People don't have the realization of just how big a jerk he really is.

> Bob Waller, broadcaster

He has the personality of a tree trunk.

> John Stearns, Mets catcher

They should've called a welder.
Richie Ashburn, Phillies broadcaster,
when Kingman's glove was being fixed, 1982

He was incredible. He could throw hard, run like a deer, and was the strongest human being I had ever seen. Didn't have a clue what the game was all about, though. He just wanted to hit the ball over the wall.
Bill Lee
The Wrong Stuff, 1984

Don't put me in the same story with that guy.
Reggie Jackson, fellow home run/strikeout artist
Sports Illustrated, 1985

The DH doesn't hurt. I'd hate to see Dave Kingman loose on the streets.
A fan, quoted in
Sport, 1985

In a way, that's pretty much a summation of Kingman's career. He strikes out on two bad pitches out of the strike zone, then hits one three blocks away.
Al Michaels
"Monday Night Baseball," ABC-TV, 1986

Chuck Klein   Hall of Fame   1934–1936

Wall Street and Mae West were the biggest busts of the Depression era. As far as the Cubs are concerned, you can add slugger Chuck Klein to that list.
Eddie Gold and Art Ahrens
The Golden Era Cubs, 1985

Gary Matthews   "Sarge"   1984–

I made a mistake trading him. . . . I make them every now and then.

Ted Turner, Braves owner

The secret to hitting, in my mind, is courage. And he has courage to burn. There is no fright in Gary.

Charlie Fox, Cubs scout

His statistics over the years don't really reflect the contributions he has made. . . . He's a very take-charge individual. That's why I named him Sarge.

Pete Rose

They call me Sarge, so I salute.

Gary Matthews
Chicago Tribune, 1984

I remember when I was a little kid and I used to sneak in Dodger Stadium. I used to change the ticket stubs, slip behind somebody, do whatever I had to do. Now, I get to play left field when I visit Dodger Stadium. That really cracks me up.

Gary Matthews
They Call Me Sarge, 1985

Why is it a player who gives so much of himself is traded so often?

Marty Noble, sportswriter, 1985

Rick Monday 1972–1976

Rick Monday, . . . a fellow Pat Boone would allow to date his daughters.

> Rick Schwab
> *Stuck on the Cubs*, 1977

If Monday meets three guys in the men's room, he thinks it's an interview and starts telling them what kind of pitch he hit.

> Tommy Lasorda, Dodgers manager
> *Inside Sports*, 1982

Tommy's the only manager in the major leagues who uses a fork for a letter opener.

> Rick Monday, on Lasorda
> *The Sporting News*, 1982

If you're going to burn the flag, don't do it in front of me. I've been to too many veterans' hospitals and seen too many broken bodies of guys who tried to protect it.

> Rick Monday, Cubs centerfielder,
> after he grabbed an American flag set on fire
> in the outfield at Dodger Stadium, 1976

Youth movements are great—if you are part of them.

> Rick Monday, on being waived
> *Sports Illustrated*, 1984

Keith Moreland 1982–

The guy can hit, but where to hide him?

> Nick Peters, Oakland *Tribune* sportswriter, 1983

Keith Moreland is a hard-working, dedicated ballplayer and an exceptional hitter. Only, someone early on neglected to teach Keith how to catch a baseball.

Havelock Hewes
Sport, 1985

The entire Cub team has given up, except for Keith Moreland, who plays each game like it's his first in the majors and the punishment for failure will be return to Triple-A. . . . Flair and natural talent [are] great, but refusal to admit defeat is greater.

Judy Aronson
Minneapolis Review of Baseball, 1985

Reporter: Why can't you catch flies like normal rightfielders?
Moreland: Because I can't get there any faster.
Keith Moreland
Chicago Cubs Souvenir Program, 1986

Bobby Murcer   1977–1979

You decide you'll wait for your pitch. Then as the ball starts toward the plate, you think about your stance. And then you think about your swing. And then you realize that the ball that went past you for a strike was your pitch.
Bobby Murcer, on batting slumps

It was nice I was invited to the Yankee welcome-home dinner. But I don't know if I'll be sitting on the dais or waiting on tables.
**Bobby Murcer, who failed to become
the next Mickey Mantle, 1982**

Billy North 1971–1972

I drilled him once before . . . that fucking hot dog!
Doug Bird, Royals pitcher, later a Cub

That might happen once out of a thousand times. Why is it you guys only remember the ones I don't get?
Billy North, to reporters after dropping a fly ball

Lou Novikoff "The Mad Russian" 1941–1944

Lou, I just figured it out. There are two ways you can play those balls. Fall down in front of them or wait until they've stopped rolling, then go after them. But remember—throw to third base, and we'll cut 'em down to doubles.
Charlie Grimm, managing Novikoff in Triple-A, 1941

He was known as the Mad Russian. He had a terrible fear of vines. As a result, he failed to catch many fly balls hit near the ivy-covered outfield walls in Wrigley Field. He also claimed that the left-field line at Wrigley was crooked.
Robbie Andreu
Fort Lauderdale News, 1985

About the only things Novikoff couldn't do were run, throw, and hit. . . . A man with an enormous amount of good nature, he had considerably less playing skill.
Bob Logan
So You Think You're a Die-Hard Cub Fan, 1985

Andy Pafko   "Pruschka"   1943–1950

If you had told me when we walked off the field that day that
it would be thirty-nine years before they won another pennant
—I wouldn't have believed you.

Andy Pafko, member of the 1945 Cubs
Sports Illustrated, 1984

I was on the first tee signing autographs, and a guy came up
to me and said he was a big fan. I had a thought. "What's
your name?" I asked. "Andy Pafko! Number Forty-Eight! I
cried when they traded you to the Dodgers!"

Tom Dreesen, comedian, 1985

Adolfo Phillips   1964–1972

He has the ability of Willie Mays, and he could make a fortune
playing baseball, if he wanted to play baseball.

Leo Durocher, Cubs manager

Paul Schramka   1953

On August 8, 1962, the Chicago Cubs officially retired Paul
Schramka's number. Ernie Banks happened to be wearing jersey number fourteen during the ceremonies at Wrigley Field.

Eddie Gold and Art Ahrens
The New Era Cubs, 1985

Frank Schulte   "Wildfire"   1904–1916

Schulte came home with the winning run like Balaam entering
Jerusalem.

Charles Van Loan, sportswriter

Billy Sunday "The Evangelist" 1883–1887

Billy Sunday was no problem—except as a batter. . . . Billy played a pretty fair game of ball, but he prayed even better.

Arthur Charles Bartlett
Baseball and Mr. Spalding, 1951

Chuck Tanner 1957–1958

When I first became manager, I asked Chuck for advice. He told me, "Always rent."

Tony LaRussa, former Cub
Seattle Post-Intelligencer, 1984

The Sporting News will always be special to baseball players. I can remember starting to read it in D-ball. You could follow our league by turning to the last page.

Chuck Tanner
Inside Sports, 1981

Frank Thomas 1960–1961, 1966

I wouldn't want him to die because I couldn't get anything for his body right now.

Casey Stengel, Mets manager
when Thomas was ill, 1963

Mike Vail 1978–1980

There isn't enough money in the world to pay me to manage if I have to look at his face every day.

Herman Franks, former Cubs manager,
calling Vail "a constant whiner," 1979

Joe Wallis "Tarzan" 1975–1978

Joe Wallis—the quarry diver, the motorcycle rider. A pistol. You know, we should have a few more of that kind of character. There are too many ballplayers reading the *Wall Street Journal* nowadays.

Jack Brickhouse, Cubs broadcaster

Before and after games he spent so much time in the clubhouse whirlpool that it was renamed the "USS Wallis."
Bob Logan
So You Think You're a Die-Hard Cub Fan, 1985

Don Young 1965, 1969

Q: In 1969, when the Cubs blew the pennant to the hated Mets, Ron Santo screamed at the Cub centerfielder because he was goofing up. Who was this unfortunate young fellow?
A: The immortal Don Young. And if I ever see him, I'll scream at him, too.

Mike Royko
Chicago Sun-Times, 1983

11. Pitchers

I'm sick of watching my pitchers get in a jam and then peeping out to the bullpen to see if a reliever is ready. I want to find out if Cub pitchers need a lantern on home plate to help them locate it.

Frankie Frisch, Cubs manager, 1950

Oh, those bases on balls.

Frankie Frisch

The bullpen is the slums of baseball. The high-rent district belongs to the Big Four starters.

Joe Garagiola, former Cubs catcher
Baseball Is a Funny Game, 1960

It was in the minor leagues. I saw a team bat around three times on Warren Hacker. Now the manager goes to take him out, and he's mad. "You can't take me out now," Hacker says. "I know I can get this guy out. I've got him out twice this inning."

Richie Ashburn, former Cubs outfielder, 1962

Some pitchers can be so tired they're practically rolling the ball in, and then when the manager asks how they feel, they'll sound like a politician a week before election day.

Rogers Hornsby
My War with Baseball, 1962

You don't save a pitcher for tomorrow. Tomorrow it may rain.

Leo Durocher, Cubs manager

I used to love the afternoon games at Wrigley Field when Gibby [Bob Gibson] pitched against our Fergie Jenkins, because you could always plan something early for that evening. They *hurried*.

Billy Williams, Cubs coach
The New Yorker, 1980

The worst animal in the world is a side-arm left-hander who wears glasses . . . and has to wipe them clean just before he throws to you.

Joe Garagiola
San Jose Mercury News, 1980

Joe Cambria [Phillies scout] even turned down Fidel Castro twice. He could have changed history if he remembered that some pitchers just mature late.

Ruben Amaro, Cubs scout

Pitchers are like a bunch of racehorses: One time they're great, the next time they're horseshit. So you have to see a pitcher a few times to get him correct.

Gary Nickels, Cub scout

I was a twenty-game winner, but it took me five years.

Dallas Green, Cubs general manager

The Chicago Cubs are living proof that weak pitching and second-division finishes go hand-in-hand.

Phil Collier
Street and Smiths Official Baseball Yearbook, 1984

Cub fans have a patent on hope. . . . Even knowing that Ken Kravec was starting against Steve Carlton, a real Cub fan would turn on the radio to find out if we won.

Jim Langford
The Cub Fan's Guide to Life, 1984

The starting pitchers we had before couldn't get anybody out. We were trying to trick the hitters. After a while, you run out of tricks.

Jody Davis, Cubs catcher, 1984

I have never met a left-handed Mexican pitcher I didn't like. They make me laugh. Don't ask me why; they just do. I look at a southpaw Mex, and I start thinking about burritos, tacos, and screwballs.

Jay Johnstone, former Cubs outfielder
Temporary Insanity, 1985

They [the relievers] wanted to know what their role is. I'd tell them, "Long and short. The longer you get 'em out, the longer you'll pitch."

Billy Connors, Cubs pitching coach
Chicago Sun-Times, 1985

The slider has kept a lot of pitchers in the big leagues, and a lot of hitters in the minor leagues.

Billy Connors
Chicago Cubs Souvenir Program, 1986

You get a game like that going and pitchers who aren't in it start to handcuff themselves to the bullpen bench or somewhere back in the clubhouse.

DeWayne Staats, as the Cubs trailed, 9–1
"Cubs Baseball," WGN-TV, 1986

Hank Aguirre   1969–1970

Aguirre was an expert on great hitters because he was one of the worst hitters.

Jay Johnstone, on the lifetime .085 hitter
Temporary Insanity, 1985

All pitchers have a license to be lousy hitters, but Hank Aguirre should have his revoked. . . . When he finally got his first hit after going o-for-two years, the fans gave him a long standing ovation.

Bruce Nash and Allan Zullo
The Baseball Hall of Shame 2, 1986

I thought hitting .333 was one hit in three years.

Hank Aguirre

Hank, you got this far . . . don't fuck it up.

**Tony Cuccinello, Indians third base coach,
when Aguirre considered stealing home, 1967**

Grover Cleveland Alexander   "Pete"   Hall of Fame 1918–1926

He'd throw you that fastball and that curve, and you couldn't tell which was which because they didn't do anything until they were right on top of you. And once they showed you what they were going to do and where they were going to do it, your bat was someplace else.

Burleigh Grimes, former pitcher

He was a loner. He would go off by himself and do what he did, which I suppose was drink.

Wild Bill Hallahan, former Cardinals teammate

Hell, I'd rather have him pitch a crucial game for me drunk than anyone I've ever known sober. He was that good.

Rogers Hornsby
My War with Baseball, 1962

He had become a multiple legend: Alexander the pitcher and Alexander the drinker. The Cubs, chronically in the second division, left him alone, even when occasionally he walked into the clubhouse listing a bit. But whatever his condition, when he went to the mound it was like Rembrandt to an easel.

> **Donald Honig**
> *Baseball America*, 1985

I liked Alec. Nice fellow. But Alec was Alec. Did he live by the rules? Sure. But they were always Alec's rules.

> **Joe McCarthy, former Cubs manager**

If we finish last again, I'd rather do it without him.

> **Joe McCarthy, before Alexander was**
> **sent to the Cardinals, 1926**

The fans marveled at how relaxed Grover Cleveland Alexander was when he was called in from the bullpen during a crucial moment of a World Series against the Yankees. He was so relaxed he was staggering. But he struck out the man [Tony Lazzeri] whether he knew it or not.

> **Mike Royko, on the 1926 Cardinals/Yankees Series**
> *Chicago Sun-Times*, 1981

What do you want me to do? Let those sons of bitches stand up there and think on my time?

> **Grover Cleveland Alexander,**
> **on why he pitched so fast**

Rich Bordi   1983–1984

I'm tired of walking through lobbies and people saying, "Who's that?"

> **Rich Bordi, after he shut out St. Louis, 1984**

Ernie Broglio   1964–1966

He had a 4–7 record in his first year with the Cubs. Before he was booed out of Chicago two years later, he won only three more games. . . . This may explain why, when he retired, he built a bonfire on his front lawn and tossed in his equipment— uniform, shoes, gloves, cap, socks, and jock strap.

Bruce Nash and Allan Zullo
The Baseball Hall of Shame, 1985

Jim Brosnan   "Professor"   1954–1958

Every time Brosnan sticks his head out of the dugout somebody hits a line drive at it.

A Cubs coach, quoted by Jim Brosnan
The Long Season, 1960

You got a sneaky fastball, though. It doesn't look as fast as it actually is. Or maybe it looks faster than it actually is.

Gene Green, Cardinals catcher

Q: A Cub relief pitcher once entered a game in a tense moment, warmed up, fell off the mound, and left the game without throwing a pitch. Name this agile creature.
A: It was the immortal Jim Brosnan. He has since become a professional writer, and he can now fall down all he wants, and nobody thinks it unusual.

Mike Royko
Chicago Sun-Times, 1983

One good pitch, good control, and a lot of nerve. Any pitcher who goes out there sixty times a season thinking he can get everybody out has to be lacking in practical common sense.

Jim Brosnan
Pennant Race, 1962

That's the best part of it.

> Jim Brosnan, when asked if the bullpen
> didn't offer a poor view of the game

Jumbo Brown 1925

He weighs two pounds more than an elephant, but that's an exaggeration—by two pounds, anyway.

> Frank Graham, New York sportswriter,
> upon first seeing the 295-pound Cubbie

He was a so-so pitcher who threw fastballs, curveballs, and the biggest shadow in baseball.

> Bruce Nash and Allan Zullo
> *The Baseball Hall of Shame 2*, 1986

Three Finger Brown   Hall of Fame   1904–1912, 1916

The team was overcome by "Three Fingered" Brown. . . . The only thing for McGraw to do to beat Chicago is to dig up a pitcher with only two fingers.

> *New York World*, 1908,
> on a crucial Giants/Cubs series

Brown lost his digital appellation the hard way—losing part of the index finger on his right hand to a corn shredder. . . . If any corn shredder ever belonged in the Hall of Fame, it was this one.

> Donald Honig
> *Baseball's 10 Greatest Teams*, 1982

Warren Brusstar   1982–1985

You can even tell which pitcher it is just from the sound of the ball hitting the catcher's glove. On the Cubs, if I hear POW! POW! POW! POW! I know Lee Smith is getting loose, but if I hear SSSSPPTT, SSSSPPTT, I know it's Warren Brusstar.

Thad Bosley, Cubs outfielder, 1986

Bob Buhl   1963–1966

He was such an awful batter that he received standing ovations for hitting foul tips.

Bruce Nash and Allan Zullo
The Baseball Hall of Shame, 1985

Lew Burdette   1964–1965

Burdette would make coffee nervous.

Fred Haney, Milwaukee Braves manager

He wouldn't admit that he threw a spitter. I said, "Heck, Lew, I used to call for it."

Tim McCarver, former catcher
The Sporting News, 1985

What makes you think I threw a spitball? All hitters are neurotic anyway. The hitters are always looking for an excuse every time they make an out. You don't hear them complaining when they hit one out of the park, do you?

Lew Burdette
Baseball Digest, 1985

Guy Bush "The Busher" 1923-1934

I was scared of Chicago. I had heard about all the gangsters and sharp men. I had never ridden an elevator that went up and down, and I didn't know about streetcars.

Guy Bush

Don Cardwell 1960-1962

Cardwell was humming so rapidly I didn't see the ball. I was swinging at the sound.

Stan Musial, Cardinals outfielder,
on Cardwell's no-hitter, 1960

Bill Caudill "The Inspector" 1979-1981

Caudill had a good arm. But I found out that he couldn't put his body down at night. History had shown here that he couldn't adapt to day games.

Lee Elia, Cubs manager
Sports Illustrated, 1982

Every club can use someone who's a little crazy.

Bobby Cox, Blue Jays manager
Chicago Tribune, 1985

Even Betty Crocker burns a cake once in a while.

Bill Caudill, after an off day
Sports Illustrated, 1982

Some guys are so easy to sucker it takes the fun out of it.

Bill Caudill, on his practical jokes
Sports Illustrated, 1982

He taught me what to do when my fastball goes: "Finesse comes in a little jar."

Bill Caudill, on Gaylord Perry
San Francisco Examiner, 1983

I'm not throwing any differently than I did in Chicago. I'm just getting the opportunity. With the Cubs, I'd work every fifth or sixth day, if I was lucky. I was the eleventh man on a ten-man staff.

Bill Caudill
Chicago Tribune, 1985

Now for the first time, October means something. Before, only my wife knew what I did in October.

Bill Caudill, making the playoffs with the Blue Jays
The Sporting News, 1985

Dave Cole 1954

That's too bad; they're the only team I can beat.

Dave Cole, sold by the Cubs to the Phillies, 1955

Jim Cosman 1970

I used to throw garbage, now I pick it up.

Jim Cosman, refuse company manager

Jim Davis 1954–1956

Jim Davis hits three ways—right-handed, left-handed, and seldom.

Pirates scouting report, on the lifetime .095 hitter

Dizzy Dean   Hall of Fame   1938–1941

Going anyplace with Dizzy was like parading behind a brass band.

Philip K. Wrigley, Cubs owner

And luck? I've always said about Dizzy Dean that if the roof fell in and Diz was sitting in the middle of the room, everybody else would be buried in the debris, and a gumdrop would drop in his mouth.

Leo Durocher
Nice Guys Finish Last, 1976

Just getting the facts from Dean was a tough job. One legendary afternoon, he claimed three different birthplaces in separate interviews with three different sportswriters. Dean said later he wanted each of them to have a story all his own.

Glenn Dickey
The History of National League Baseball, 1979

Them ain't lies. Them's scoops.

Dizzy Dean

Diz just says whatever comes into his head—even if it's nothing.

Anon., on Dean's job as a broadcaster

We had no control over what he'd do each week. I'd sit there in front of the television and cringe.

Bill MacPhail, CBS Sports

The game began and you were "podner" once more. Dean made you laugh. He made you listen. He made life gentle. He let you love.

> **Curt Smith**
> *American's Dizzy Dean*, 1978

He resurfaced as a radio and then television announcer, popular, well-paid, spectacularly ungrammatical, handling the language like a spastic juggling raw eggs.

> **Donald Honig**
> *Baseball America*, 1985

It's pretty nice for an ol' Arkansas cotton picker to be up here with these city boys. The Good Lord was good to me. He gave me a strong body, a good right arm, and a weak mind.

> **Dizzy Dean, at his Hall of Fame induction, 1953**

Diz was a kid to the end.

> **Pee Wee Reese, former Dodgers shortstop, 1974**

Moe Drabowsky   1956–1960

I didn't see it, but it sounded low.

> **Jim King, Cubs outfielder,**
> **taking batting practice from Drabowsky, 1956**

Baseball needs more nuts like you.

> **Letter from young boy, Keokuk, Iowa, 1966**

There is no bigger flake in organized baseball than Drabowsky. Once, out in the bullpen in Anaheim, he picked up the phone, called a number in Hong Kong and ordered a Chinese dinner. To go.

Jim Bouton
Ball Four, 1971

Some losers throw chairs. Drabowsky threw rooms. One of his worst tantrums cost him a bundle after a particularly tough loss on the road. Drabowsky stormed back to the team's hotel and went ten rounds with his room. The room lost.

Bruce Nash and Allan Zullo
The Baseball Hall of Shame, 1985

I was a mediocre ballplayer, sure. . . . But don't forget, Drabowsky was the second Polack to appear in a World Series. The first one carried a rake.

Moe Drabowsky

Dick Drott "Hummer" 1957–1961

Dick has the killer instinct of a tiger and the friendliness of a lamb.

Bob Scheffing, Cubs manager, 1957

Dennis Eckersley 1984–

Dennis Eckersley . . . looks more like an aged and blissed-out hippie who has lost his way and somehow found himself in a major league game.

Skip Myslenski and Linda Kay
Chicago Tribune, 1984

He has had some year. I'd be afraid lightning would strike me if I pitched as well as he has.

Dennis Eckersley, on Rick Sutcliffe's 16–1 record
Chicago Tribune, 1984

I can give up home runs anywhere.

Dennis Eckersley, comparing
Fenway Park to Wrigley Field, 1984

I know I only need one more complete game for one hundred. Who cares? That macho complete-game bull is overrated.

Dennis Eckersley
Baseball Digest, 1985

Darcy Fast   1968

What a great name for a pitcher! But the truth is the only thing fast about Darcy was his career (0–1 in eight games) for the '68 Cubs.

Rich Marazzi and Len Fiorito
Aaron to Zippel, 1985

Bill Faul   1965–1966

Bill was the craziest guy I ever met or heard of. With the possible exception of the Marquis de Sade, there was nobody else in his league.

Bill Lee
The Wrong Stuff, 1984

He prepared for games by biting the heads off live parakeets. He also swallowed live toads, claiming they put an extra hop on his fastball.

Robbie Andreu
Fort Lauderdale News, 1985

Faul . . . should have tried hypnotizing the batters instead of himself.

> **Bob Logan**
> *So You Think You're a Die-Hard Cub Fan*, 1985

George Frazier 1984–1986

Frazier . . . earned no compassion from the crowd. They booed his entrance lustily. The miracle was that any of them was awake enough to notice.

> **Phil Hersh**
> *Chicago Tribune*, 1986

Everybody says that Frazier has great stuff. You'd have to agree. But they sure get an awful lot of hits off him for the innings he pitches.

> **Harry Caray**
> "Cubs Baseball," WGN-TV, Chicago, 1986

The guy is so inept, for Pete's sakes. You would think he would have wanted to sneak out of town. . . . They paid him so much money he was able to buy a racing stable, and I bet his horses aren't going good, either.

> **Harry Caray, after Frazier was traded**
> "Cubs Baseball," WGN-TV, Chicago, 1986

I have a lot of movement on the ball, but I don't know where it's going. I threw one to Tony Perez the other night that started down the middle, but almost hit him.

> **George Frazier**
> *Chicago Sun-Times*, 1985

Long relief is like being a plumber. Some days it's okay, but when thirty septic tanks back up, it's no fun.

> **George Frazier**
> *Sports Illustrated,* 1985

I don't put any foreign substances on the baseball. Everything I use on it is from the good ol' U.S.A.

> **George Frazier**
> *Sports Illustrated,* 1985

Larry French 1935–1941

When I looked around, I didn't know whether I was pitching for the whites or grays.

> **Larry French, after beating Pittsburgh 3–2,**
> **but leaving thirteen men on base**

Clark Griffith "The Old Fox" Hall of Fame
1893–1900

How else were you going to get "Shoeless Joe" Jackson out?

> **Clark Griffith, on the spitball**

Burleigh Grimes "Ol' Stubblebeard" Hall of Fame
1932–1933

Batters trembled just looking at Grimes. He didn't shave before games, so thick stubble blackened his glowering face. . . . Ol' Stubblebeard, who learned to throw a spitter and a duster before he was old enough to grow whiskers, was happiest when he made batters eat dirt.

> **Bruce Nash and Allan Zullo**
> *Baseball Hall of Shame 2,* 1986

Goose [Goslin] was so eager to get back up there and bat he was inching out of the batter's circle. So I let him have it.
Burleigh Grimes, on his beaning of an on-deck hitter

Some days that's all I threw. It got 'em real upset.
Burleigh Grimes, on the spitter
Minneapolis Review of Baseball, 1985

Billy Gumpert   1985–

He's in trouble; that was my number with the Cubs.
Billy Connors, Cubs coach, on Gumpert's number 45
Chicago Sun-Times, 1985

Ed Hanyzewski   1942–1946

I liked to have broken my jaw tryin' to pronounce that one. But I said his name by just holdin' my nose and sneezing.
Dizzy Dean, broadcaster

Kirby Higbe   1937–1939

It's dangerous to be on the same field Hig is pitching on.
**Rube Marquard, Tulsa Triple-A manager,
on his wildness, 1933**

He thinks left-handed, and his left arm gets sore, too.
**Andy Lotshaw, Cubs trainer,
on why he rubs up Higbe's left arm, 1938**

I have always had good luck. The only bad luck I have had, I have brought on myself.
Kirby Higbe
The High Hard One, 1967

I developed my strong right arm early in life by getting in rock fights and by making bets I could throw rocks farther than anybody thought any boy ever could. I didn't know then that in later life my right arm would be my sole means of support.

Kirby Higbe
The High Hard One, 1967

Ken Holtzman 1965–1971, 1978–1979

I hate this ballpark. It stinks. I don't ever want to pitch here again or anywhere else for the Cubs.

Ken Holtzman, before being traded to the A's, 1971

I'll give you an exclusive. . . . Holtzman is the most miserable man I have met in baseball. Holtzman was with the Chicago Cubs, and he hated it there. We had him in Oakland, and he hated it. . . . He hates himself.

Charlie Finley, Oakland A's owner

Finley thinks he knows baseball, but I don't think he knows that much about the game.

Ken Holtzman

Burt Hooten "Happy" 1971–1975

To put it mildly, Hooten was a bust as a Cub. . . . Sometimes his knuckle curve acted more like a nickel curve. And the extra flab didn't help him on the slab.

Eddie Gold and Art Ahrens
The New Era Cubs, 1985

He became Happy Hooten on New Year's Eve. Normally, he looks about as happy as a farmer during a drought, but when I caught him playing solitaire during a New Year's celebration, he earned his nickname, and he's been Happy ever since.

Tommy Lasorda
The Artful Dodger, 1986

Ferguson Jenkins   1967–1973, 1982–1983

Fergie was traded to Texas [from the Red Sox] for a couple of used baseballs and an autographed picture of Roy Rogers and Dale Evans.

Bill Lee, on Jenkins' trade for John Poloni and cash
The Wrong Stuff, 1984

The Ferguson Jenkins Award: Given to the best pitcher on the worst team, the guy who has little chance to win the Cy Young because his team can't stay in a pennant race past Memorial Day.

Tom Weir
USA Today, 1984

After you've given up a home run it gets very lonely on the pitcher's mound. None of the infielders wants to share the spotlight with you. Forget about your catcher, he's trying to pretend he doesn't even know you.

Ferguson Jenkins, 1983

Mike Krukow   1976–1981

It's like Noah's wife told him. She said, "Noah, honey, it's going to stop raining one of these days."

Mike Krukow, after a 21–3 loss to the Cardinals
Sports Illustrated, 1977

They'll boo you if you don't cover first. They'll boo you if you don't back up a base. In Philadelphia, they'll boo you just to stay in shape.

> **Mike Krukow, on life after the Cubs**
> *San Jose Mercury News*, 1982

Dennis Lamp   1977–1980

I guess I'd better send my fingers to Cooperstown.

> **Dennis Lamp, after Lou Brock**
> **got hit number 3,000 off his pitching hand, 1979**

Grover Loudermilk   "Slim"   1912

When Loudermilk went in to pitch, perhaps anything could happen, but one thing usually did occur. Batters walked to first base. . . . Quite obviously he threw strikes, but I can't remember them.

> **James T. Farrell**
> *My Baseball Diary*, 1957

Carl Lundgren   1902–1909

The "Human Icicle" was one of the most careful observers of batters ever found. He was of the type that studies three aces and a pair of tens for two minutes before calling. . . . When he calls, he wins, and he pitched wonderful ball for Chicago.

> **Johnny Evers**
> *Baseball in the Big Leagues*, 1910

Lindy McDaniel 1963–1965

McDaniel didn't drink, didn't smoke, and didn't cuss. In addition, he carried a Bible. . . . He was possibly the only preacher with a great knockdown pitch.

Eddie Gold and Art Ahrens
The New Era Cubs, 1985

Lynn McGlothen 1978–1981

If I threw like Lynn, I wouldn't want to put the ball over the plate either.

Dave Kingman, Mets infielder,
after McGlothen said he'd knock down Kingman, 1981

Cal McLish "Buster" 1949, 1951

Would you give me a little less motion and a little more ball?

His catcher

Pat Malone 1928–1934

It was a big gamble to give him the sacrifice sign. More than once he bunted into a double play. A lazy trot, for Pat, was full speed.

Charlie Grimm
Jolly Cholly's Story, 1968

I remember Pat Malone, a sidearmer for the Cubs. He'd pitch you here [inside] and your ass left in a hurry.

Leo Durocher, former Cubs manager
Cubs Vine Line, 1986

Randy Martz 1980–1982

We knew about Martz—never worked, never did a goddamn thing to keep himself in shape. With day baseball he's down there on Rush Street all night.

Dallas Green, Cubs president
Chicago Magazine, 1985

Dickie Noles 1982–1984

We pitchers, we're all weirdos. Everything that ever happens, happens to help the hitters. Move in the fences, juice up the baseball. But us weirdos, all we got out there on the mound is our resin bag.

Dickie Noles
Inside Sports, 1982

Milt Pappas "Gimpy" 1970–1973

The starting pitcher tomorrow for the Cubs will be Milt Pappas, *if* they can talk him into it.

Vince Lloyd, after the Cubs lost ten straight
"Cubs Baseball," WGN-Radio, Chicago, 1973

Mike Proly 1982–1983

I'm not going to agree with them, and I'm not going to deny it. I do have a tendency to go to my hat a lot. . . . That's not where it is, though.

Mike Proly, on the spitter
Sports Illustrated, 1983

Phil Regan "The Vulture" 1968–1972

My daddy always told me, "If you're going to war, take all your weapons."

> **Phil Regan, asked if he used a spitter**
> *Chicago Sun-Times*, 1985

Rick Reuschel 1972–1981, 1983–1984

Decker: The Reuschel brothers—whale number one and whale number two. Humpty and Dumpty.
Zig: Tweedle Dum and Tweedle Dumber.
Decker: They're good pitchers, but they're built like turnips.

> **Organic Theatre Company**
> *Bleacher Bums*, 1977

You pitched ten years in Chicago, and nobody ever heard of you. Now, you're a Yankee, and you get one little blister on your hand, and you can't pitch in the Championship Series, and all of a sudden you're famous. That's the way it is in New York, kiddo.

> **Joe Garagiola**
> "American League Championship Series," NBC-TV, 1981

It was a family in New York, but I didn't enjoy Papa [George Steinbrenner].

> **Rick Reuschel, returning to the Cubs**
> *Sports Illustrated*, 1984

Allen Ripley 1982

I've watched you spend a half hour getting three guys out a number of times already this season, and now you want to start a game? Well, Allen, I'm not sure anyone on this club has got that much time to watch you work five innings.

> **Lee Elia, Cubs manager, 1982**

Freddy Rodriguez   1958

Q: Name at least one Cub pitcher of the 1950s who wore a golden earring.
A: The immortal Fernando Pedro Rodriguez. He didn't lose a game in 1958. But he didn't win any, either.

> **Mike Royko**
> *Chicago Sun-Times,* 1983

Dick Ruthven   "Rufus"   1983–1986

Ruthven, a man of few words, and even fewer pitches.

> **Peter Pascarelli**
> *Philadelphia Inquirer,* 1983

Scott Sanderson   1984–

Scott Sanderson . . . comes from prissy Northbrook, one of those suburbs where the car mechanics speak German. Sanderson is tall and lean and so good-looking that he is almost pretty. He went off to Vanderbilt University, which wasn't named for a rich man for nothing.

> **Phil Hersh**
> *Inside Sports,* 1985

Stone: Would you describe Sanderson's style as deliberate?
Caray: You can tell he doesn't have an attendance clause in his contract.

> **Steve Stone and Harry Caray, on a game called by darkness**
> "Cubs Baseball," WGN-TV, Chicago, 1986

They ought to put lights in Wrigley Field just for Sanderson's games.

> **Arne Harris, producer/director**
> "Cubs Baseball," WGN-TV, Chicago, 1986

I'm not getting paid to get people home for dinner on time. I'm getting paid to win ballgames.

Scott Sanderson
Chicago Tribune, 1986

Bob Shaw 1967

I've got to find out whether he is the lousiest lay in the world or the cheapest son of a bitch in baseball. Why else wouldn't a girl date him twice?

Al Lopez, White Sox manager

I noticed right away that some of his pitches traveled to the plate in a very unnatural way. My eyes near clean popped from my head. I knew how Tom Edison felt when he discovered the electric light. Bob Shaw promptly became my idol.

Gaylord Perry
Me and the Spitter, 1974

Lee Smith 1980–

They should make Lee Smith pitch from second base.

George Hendrick, Cardinals outfielder

I don't run from anybody, but the general opinion around the National League is that you're in no real hurry to get to him.

Dusty Baker
The Sporting News, 1983

Lee is saved for saves, and the Cubs are beyond saving.

Ray Sons
Chicago Sun-Times, 1985

Eddie Solomon   "Buddy"   1975

Eddie Solomon took umbrage at a writer in the clubhouse and threw a chair at him. Naturally, the chair sailed high and outside.

Bob Verdi
Chicago Tribune, 1975

Albert G. Spalding   Hall of Fame   1876–1878

Clubs come to Chicago and spit on their hands with ferocity and explain that they are going to "knock the stuffing out of Spalding" because "anybody can hit him; he is the easiest man in the business." And they don't do it all the same.

Chicago Tribune, 1876

Steve Stone   1974–1976

Funny thing is, a couple of months later, he hit the top of the wall against me. How would that have looked on my record?
Steve Stone, on Duane Kuiper, whose only homer in 3,378 at bats came against Stone, 1985

Players fainted in the dugout. The pitcher just stood on the mound looking at the spot the ball had landed, probably trying to decide what he wanted to do after baseball.

Ron Luciano, on Kuiper's home run
The Fall of the Roman Umpire, 1986

In pitching or in restaurants, it's the same story: location.
Steve Stone
"Cubs Baseball," WGN-TV, Chicago, 1986

Rick Sutcliffe "The Red Baron" 1984–

As far as he's reaching for that fastball, he's liable to catch his hand in Manny Trillo's belt.

Lon Simmons
"A's Baseball," KSFO-Radio, San Francisco, 1983

If Sutcliffe takes this long to pitch every inning, your hair will be out of style, Wayne.

Lon Simmons, to his fellow broadcaster Wayne Hagen
"A's Baseball," KSFO-Radio, San Francisco, 1983

If this was a ship named *Titanic,* I wonder how many of our people would let the women and children off first.

Rick Sutcliffe, before leaving the Indians
Seattle Times, 1984

Some people believe we have a strange force in the sky who wants the Cubs to win. Actually, we have a 6'7" guy who throws the hell out of the ball. . . . *That's* our strange force.

Jim Frey, Cubs manager
Sports Illustrated, 1984

Joining the team that beat Sutcliffe in the last Cub game of the year would be as tasteless as an accused murderer marrying the victim's widow.

Bernie Lincicome, on rumors of going to the Padres
Chicago Tribune, 1984

I heard the Royals tried everything to get Sutcliffe except kidnap him.

**George Brett, Royals infielder,
on Sutcliffe's free-agency**
Kansas City Star, 1985

Just because he was 16–1 last year doesn't make him God.

> Ron Darling, Mets pitcher
> *The Sporting News*, 1985

He's deliberate; he almost leers at the hitter. Crowd the plate, and he's not reluctant to play some chin music. At the end of each inning he doesn't walk off the mound—no, Rick Sutcliffe struts.

> Michael K. Herbert
> *Inside Sports*, 1985

Bruce Sutter   1976–1980

I don't think Johnny Carson got a lot of hate mail when he signed for $5 million. But Bruce Sutter probably did. Why? Well, Johnny's a lot funnier than Bruce. I mean, Bruce is a wonderful guy, but his Karnak is weak.

> Steve Stone, Orioles pitcher, 1981

The Cardinals have decided not to play fair anymore; they brought in Bruce Sutter.

> Hank Greenwald
> "Giants Baseball," KNBR-Radio, San Francisco, 1982

He's willing to talk, but he lacks color and flair. His interviews were very similar to his pitching appearances. Thorough, efficient, and bland. I couldn't get any hits off him.

> Jerry Green, *Detroit News* columnist, 1983

Playing behind him in my first two years with the Cubs, he was the biggest mismatch I have ever seen. He made good hitters miss by two feet.

> Bill Buckner, Red Sox infielder
> *Baseball Digest*, 1984

Whenever hitters get together and talk about Bruce Sutter, they are like fishermen gathered in a tavern after a day on the lake. They savor every hit as if it were a world-record trophy.

Robert Markus
Baseball Digest, 1984

I hold Bruce Sutter personally responsible for my .245 average. When I came up, I was programmed on two pitches: the fastball and slider. Now kids come up throwing 2–0 forkballs. I can't even hit our eighteen-year-olds in spring training anymore.

Bill Madlock, Dodgers infielder
USA Today, 1985

Only God can save forty-five games, and now he's gone to Atlanta.

Neil Allen, Cardinals pitcher
Sport, 1985

The split-finger did everything for my career. If it wasn't for that pitch, I'd be back in Pennsylvania working in a printer's shop.

Bruce Sutter, taught it by the Cubs' Fred Martin
Sports Illustrated, 1986

Steve Trout "Rainbow" 1983–

Steve Trout, whose father's name, Dizzy, must have been passed on genetically.

Phil Hersh
Chicago Sun-Times, 1982

There should be a common sense clause in his contract.

Jim Frey, after Trout fell off a bicycle and was injured
Sports Illustrated, 1986

Rick Sutcliffe was the big fish the Chicago Cubs reeled in last winter, but it appears Steve Trout was a pretty good catch, too.

Associated Press, 1985

Steve Trout no longer is on a fishing expedition to find himself as a pitcher. He has learned that batters will fall hook and line for his sinker.

Phil Hersh
Chicago Tribune, 1985

My father was a giver. He had a large family, seven sons and three daughters—I guess you could say we were a "school of trout."

Steve Trout
Cubs Vine Line, 1986

Oscar Zamora 1974–1976

When the pitch is so fat
That the ball hits the bat—
That's Zamora.

Wrigley Field song, 1970s

12. The Press

I became convinced that—as far as baseball is concerned—good, liberal roasts in newspapers of wide circulation are much more effective than fulsome praise.

Albert G. Spalding, White Stockings owner, c. 1880s.

The Iron Man [Joe McGinnity] has zinc in his curves and Evers hit one. It rose and came right down in Shannon's hands, but just as the ball arrived Shannon thoughtfully turned his back and fled. The sun had blinded him and he feared that the ball would fall on the vacuum that terminated his neck.

W. A. Phelon, reporting on the Cubs versus Giants
Chicago Journal, 1908

Scoring . . . is a source of much pleasure, for on long winter evenings, sitting near the cheerful size of a hard-working radiator, I can draw out the score books of long ago, and have another game.

Hugh S. Fullerton, Chicago sportswriter, 1910

A ballplayer has two reputations, one with the players and one with the fans. The first is based on ability. The second the newspapers give him.

Johnny Evers, former Cubs infielder, 1925

Baseball writers as a rule are by no means abnormal. Some people even say they are human. . . . Some baseball writers write with a stiletto dipped in their own venomous bile.

Jim Brosnan
The Long Season, 1960

The sportswriter, who usually can't raise five dollars without borrowing or going home.

Rogers Hornsby
My War with Baseball, 1962

You say I haven't gotten the publicity I deserve over the years, and that I'm an underrated player. Well, that's up to you guys. I can't write about myself.

Billy Williams, Cubs outfielder, 1969

Naw, I make 'em up like everyone else.
> **Dave Kingman, Cubs outfielder, when asked if he**
> **used a tape recorder for his baseball column, 1978**

They can write what they want. Most of it is bull, anyway. If they can't find legitimate stories, they'll make one up.
> **Rick Reuschel, Cubs pitcher**

One of the worst aspects of being a sportswriter is that you get older and the athletes get younger.
> **Jerome Holtzman, Chicago sportswriter**
> *The New Yorker*, 1979

You get tired of saying the same thing. It's like Lindbergh—he spent ten fucking years talking to people about flying across the ocean.
> **Jim Frey, future Cubs manager, 1980**

Now you've got something to write about for two days.
> **Dave Kingman, Cubs outfielder,**
> **dumping a bucket of water on a sportswriter, 1980**

It could be worse. Let's face it, it's a lot better than getting up at five A.M. and working in a pickle factory.
> **Bob Logan, on covering the Cubs**
> *San Jose Mercury News*, 1981

The Chicago press wouldn't know a ballplayer if they fell over one.
> **Dallas Green, Cubs general manager**

If I can stand sixty feet six inches from Steve Garvey and face him, I can face you from two feet and answer your questions.
**George Frazier, future Cubs pitcher,
on dealing with press after a bad day, 1982**

This fouls up our playoff rotation.
**Ned Colletti, Cubs assistant public relations director,
after the opener was rained out, 1983**

This is the biggest story in Chicago since Mayor Daley died.
**Steve Daley (no relation), Chicago sportswriter,
on the Cubs success, 1984**

No cause for alarm. Alarm is created up there in the press box, not down on the field.
**Randy Hundley, former Cubs catcher,
when asked if the Cubs might fold, 1984**

You can't win a division by twelve games without bats. If I tell you that the toughest game to win in a short series is the last game, it's not even worth writing down. Hey, you're writing it down.
George Frazier, Cubs pitcher, on the playoffs
Chicago Tribune, 1984

I never let business interfere with passion.
**George Will, on why he watched the Cubs instead
of brushing up for the presidential debate, 1984**

If you had a date with the first-runner up at the Miss Universe pageant, you'd complain about not getting number one.
**Jonathan Bone, letter to Chicago sportswriter
Bernie Lincicome, 1985**

You think ballplayers are nomads? Try keeping track of one of those guys [sportswriters]. At least the clubhouse is my home on the road. Those guys live with only two burning questions: Can I make deadline, and what time does the bar close? Their official stationery is a cocktail napkin.

Jay Johnstone
Temporary Insanity, 1985

You've got to try to win the game whether it's hot or cold. In two months, you'll be asking me if it is too hot. A month ago, you asked me if it was too cold. Today, it was too wet.

Jim Frey, Cubs manager, to reporters
Chicago Tribune, 1985

How can sportswriters criticize me when most of 'em are fat. They just sit around here and watch us do exercises. How can they say I'm not working hard?

Dave Kingman, still complaining about the press
Seattle Post-Intelligencer, 1986

13. Broadcast Media

In sports broadcasting, we have some of the world's mealiest mealymouths. If a . . . player ever whipped out a switchblade and cut the throat of an opposing player, the announcer would probably say, "Well, there's a little temper flare-up down there."

Mike Royko
Chicago Sun-Times, 1981

They go head-to-head against the networks' best prime-time tearjerkers, and top them all in anguish, heartbreak, dashed hopes, disappointment, and men left on base.

Glen Waggoner, on the Cubs on WGN-TV
Sport, 1984

When people come to my house and we watch the Cubs, I tell them to talk baseball or get out.

Chuck Connors, former Cubs infielder
Bill Mazeroski's Baseball, 1985

One might have thought Wrigley Field had been converted into an amusement park or that Ryne Sandberg had defected to the Soviet Union.

Norman Chad, Washington reporter, after a
Maryland cable network dropped WGN-TV, 1985

Don't move. I want to get some TV exposure.

Leon Durham, Cubs first baseman,
after Pete Rose got hit number 4,191, 1985

Jack Brickhouse   Cubs Broadcaster   Hall of Fame
1940–1943, 1947–1981

Jack Brickhouse has seen more bad baseball than any person, living or dead.

Steve Daley
Chicago Tribune

Jack has a knack of never irritating his interviewee by disagreeing with him or asking controversial questions . . . or listening to what he says.

Rick Schwab
Stuck on the Cubs, 1977

This book is for Jack Brickhouse, a winner, even when the Cubs were losing.

> Bob Logan
> *Cubs Win!*, 1984

Ladies and gentlemen, here's Hall of Famer Jack Brickhouse. . . . Do you realize that tens of thousands of people grew up not knowing anything about football because they listened to Jack Brickhouse and Irv Kupcinet on the Bears broadcast?

> **Tom Dreesen, comedian, WGN-TV banquet, 1985**

He never gave in to the Cosell revolution of investigative journalism. He never felt that need to wear a Nehru jacket or a double-breasted Edwardian when the six-year-old blue blazer only had one mustard stain.

> **Chet Coppock, sports broadcaster**
> *Cubs Vine Line*, 1986

I'll straighten out world affairs the first two hours, then stretch out the third hour talking about baseball.

> **Jack Brickhouse, on his Hall of Fame speech**
> *The Sporting News*, 1983

I stand this day on what I consider the hallowed baseball ground of Cooperstown. I feel at this moment like a man who is sixty feet six inches tall.

> **Jack Brickhouse, Hall of Fame induction speech, 1983**

There's an old saying—if you steal from one person it's plagiarism, but if you steal from enough, it's research. As a sports broadcaster for years, I've been an ardent "researcher."

> **Jack Brickhouse**

Back she goes . . . Way back! . . . Back! . . . Back! . . . Hey!
Hey!

Jack Brickhouse, his home run call

Lou Boudreau Cubs Broadcaster 1958–1959, 1961–

No doubt about it.

Lou Boudreau, his home run call

Harry Caray Cubs Broadcaster 1982–

The only thing bigger than Harry's popularity in Chicago these days is his ego. Like Howard Cosell, he is a legend in his own mind.

Rick Schwab, when Caray was broadcasting the White Sox
Stuck on the Cubs, 1977

I tell it like it is. Cosell tells it like Roone Arledge wants it told.

Harry Caray

He could take the parting of the Red Sea and make it last four hours.

Steve Stone, Cubs broadcaster
San Francisco Examiner, 1983

Caray, whose distinctive voice sounds like he is trying to wash down a mouthful of pebbles with Bromo Seltzer.

Phil Hersh
Inside Sports, 1985

In this sun-baked, bare-backed heaven of beer and sweat and tattoos, Harry is Santa Claus in August—only the red radiating from Caray comes from a crimson, luau-size Hawaiian shirt. It drapes his bowl-of-pudding belly and gives way to a pair of Bermuda shorts.

Bill Brashler
Chicago Sun-Times, 1985

He's just like the other fans, except that he probably drinks more beer during the game than they do.

William E. Geist
Esquire, 1985

Cubs win. Of course, if I was Harry Caray, I would have said, "Cubs win!!" about six times at the top of my lungs.

Bob Costas
"Game of the Week," NBC-TV, 1986

A million-dollar tan for three bucks. When this isn't fun anymore, I'll get out.

Harry Caray

The fans aren't looking for a Pavarotti or some golden-throated tenor from the Metropolitan Opera. They accept me because I talk like a fan, think like a fan, and react like a fan. These are my people, and we talk the same language—baseball.

Harry Caray

So I wouldn't say something unprintable on the air by accident.

Harry Caray, on why he adopted the phrase "Holy Cow!"

I started in broadcasting in 1945 doing the Cardinals and saying "Holy Cow." That Rizzuto was just a shortstop. . . . "Holy Cow" is mine.
> **Harry Caray, on Phil Rizzuto's theft of the phrase**
> *Chicago Sun-Times,* 1985

Listen, David, you've never succeeded in this business until you've had the experience of working with a terrific hangover. Not until then, when you've been able to come through with flying colors under those circumstances, can you consider yourself a professional. And Lord knows I've had more than my share of hangovers. But I've never missed a day, folks. Never missed a night, either.
> **Harry Caray**
> "Late Night With David Letterman," NBC-TV, 1986

There's nothing like fun at the old ballpark.
> **Harry Caray**

It might be, it could be, it is!
> **Harry Caray, his home run call**

Leo Durocher   Cubs Radio Show

As for Leo, there was happiness in knowing his show was a service to baseball fans. There was security in knowing he won ninety-five percent of the arguments concerning his baseball strategy, even if half of his callers were twelve-year-olds.
> **Rick Schwab**
> *Stuck on the Cubs,* 1977

Who ever heard of a guy from Brooklyn needing a mike?
> **Leo Durocher**
> *Sport,* 1947

Milo Hamilton   Cubs Broadcaster   1980–1984

Hamilton as a broadcaster is a model of professionalism, fluency, and deportment; he is, in short, as interesting as the weather channel. . . . He broadcasts baseball games in a tone that would be more appropriate for a man reviewing a loan application.

Bill James
The Bill James Baseball Abstract, 1985

Milo Hamilton's ego just consumed him.

Harry Caray, on Hamilton's dismissal
"Chicago Tonight," WTTW-Radio, Chicago, 1985

Brickhouse used to brag about how well I did my homework . . . but Caray used to ridicule it, saying fans don't want all those stats. I think they'd rather have stats than the names of two hundred tavern operators.

Milo Hamilton
Inside Sports, 1985

Vince Lloyd   Cubs Broadcaster   1965–

Holy Mackerel!

Vince Lloyd, his home run call

Pat Pieper   Cubs Field Announcer   1914–1974

He was known for his drawn-out cry of "Play ball!" which he delivered immediately after giving the lineups. Pieper was to Cub fans what Ed McMahon is to Johnny Carson.

Dan Schlossberg
The Baseball Catalog, 1980

Jimmy Piersall   Chicago Sports Talk Host

The best thing that ever happened to me was going nuts. Nobody knew me until I went nuts. Now, when I walk in downtown Chicago, the majority of people know me.

Jimmy Piersall
Chicago Sun-Times, 1984

You wish this peevish, self-righteous, caterwauling brat would grow up and put a lid on it once in a while.

Bill Brashler
Chicago Magazine, 1985

Jack Quinlan   Cubs Broadcaster   1958–1965

Jack Quinlan and WGN formed an unforgettable parlay. Quinlan had the big sound, the sound which has brought the station greatness. His voice possessed the firmness of a hearty handshake. The resonance of a finely tuned harp. The clarity of a starry night. The quality of a prayer.

Jack Rosenberg, sports editor,
delivering the eulogy, 1965

Ronald W. Reagan   Cubs Broadcaster

Ronald Reagan has had the two most demanding jobs in the country—President of the United States and radio broadcaster for the Chicago Cubs.

George Will
Washington Post

I knew of only one thing that wouldn't get me in the score column and betray me—a foul ball. So I had Augie Galan foul this pitch down the left field foul line. He fouled for six minutes and forty-five seconds until I lost count. I began to be frightened that maybe I was establishing a new world record for a fellow staying at bat hitting fouls.

> **Ronald W. Reagan, broadcasting a game**
> **when the telegraphic wire went dead**

DeWayne Staats   Cubs Broadcaster   1985–

It didn't sink until it got into the bleachers.

> **DeWayne Staats, on a homer off sinkerballer**
> **Roger McDowell, 1985**

That ball has got a chance. Way back! Gone!

> **DeWayne Staats, his home run call**

Steve Stone   Cubs Broadcaster   1983–

Caray: A bouncing ball up the middle—Oquendo cannot come up with it, because he stands only five-foot seven.
Stone: Harry, he was just playing him too low.

> **Steve Stone**
> **"Cubs Baseball," WGN-TV, 1986**

You can forget it, it's long gone.

> **Steve Stone, his home run call**

Bert Wilson   Cubs Broadcaster   1943–1955

Bert really lived and died with the Cubs. He often said, "When I die, just bury me in the bullpen."

> **Jack Brickhouse, Cubs broadcaster**

Uncle Bert was the optimistic sort. Although his beloved Cubbies could be a dozen runs behind, Wilson would always say "the game is never over until the last man is out." That was the sure signal to flip the dial.

Eddie Gold
Cubs Vine Line, 1986

We don't care who wins—as long as it's the Cubs.

Bert Wilson

If you like the Cubs, I make sense. If you don't, you won't tune in.

Bert Wilson

14. The Summer Game

Baseball owes its prestige as our national game to the fact that no other form of sport is such an exponent of American courage, confidence, combativeness, dash, discipline, determination, energy, eagerness, pluck, persistency, performance, spirit, sagacity, success, vim, vigor, and virility.

Albert G. Spalding
America's National Game, 1911

Baseball and malaria keep coming back.

Gene Mauch, former Cubs infielder

Between the foul lines is a world in which the highest laws of civilization and the most fundamental laws of the jungle apply. Each player is alone, and they are all working together.

Joe Garagiola
Baseball Is a Funny Game, 1960

Baseball is really a simple game. It's a game you have to play by ear.

Richie Ashburn, former Cubs outfielder

Brickhouse: If all the sports broadcasters and all the baseball owners and all the garbage collectors in the world were to go on strike, which one do you think would be missed first?
Cosell: The garbage collectors.
Brickhouse: Of course. Let's take it from there.

Jack Brickhouse and Howard Cosell
"Kup's Show," WMAQ-TV, Chicago, 1974

That's what's good about baseball. You can do something about yesterday tomorrow.

Manny Trillo, former Cubs infielder
San Francisco Examiner, 1979

Baseball frees us from a winter spent leaning into a thirty-mile-per-hour wind at a bus stop, which is why we love it so.

Steve Daley
Chicago Tribune, 1984

Nobody knows as much about this game as they think.

Jim Frey, Cubs manager, 1984

There are very few businesses that sell dreams. Baseball is one of them. When you come away from a ballgame, you have nothing but the ephemeral idea that you had a good time.

Bill Veeck
Chicago Magazine, 1985

I remember one time we were having dinner, and my sister, Dana—she was about eight or nine at the time—interrupted the conversation and said, "Baseball, baseball. Why can't we talk about something besides baseball."

Roy Smalley, Jr., whose father was a Cub
Chicago Tribune, 1985

The mind game, that was the beauty of it.

Lou Brock
Baseball Digest, 1985

Other sports are just sports. Baseball is a love.

Bryant Gumbel, television host and Cubs fan

It has been said that baseball is to the United States what revolutions are to Latin America, a safety valve for letting off steam. I think baseball is more serious than any Latin American revolution. But, then, I am a serious fan. How serious? I like *Sports Illustrated*'s baseball issue even more than its swimsuit issue.

George Will
Newsweek, 1985

I wish George Will did more sports stuff in his nationally syndicated column (he knows more about sports than politics, anyhow).

Larry King
The Sporting News, 1984

The guy's terrific. Brilliant. He could run for office. His only problem is he's a Cubs fan.

Warner Wolf, on George Will
Gimme a Break!, 1983

Why is it there are so many nice guys interested in baseball? Not me. I was a real bastard when I played.

> **Burleigh Grimes, former Cubs pitcher**
> *Minneapolis Review of Baseball*, 1985

If these [old] parks go, it won't be the end of Western civilization, but it will be one giant step toward the homogenization of all of us. When there is no room for individualism in ballparks, there will be no room for individualism in life.

> **Bill Veeck**
> *Baseball Digest*, 1985

Have you noticed they don't have ticket-sellers anymore? There are no more peddlers. Everybody is a vice-president of marketing these days.

> **Bill Veeck**
> *Chicago Tribune*, 1985

People come to baseball games to study the quantitative method of optimum decision-making under conditions of uncertainty. It ameliorates the classic polarization between the self-motivated individual and the collective ideology.

> **Ernie Banks, speaking in Vero Beach, Florida**
> *USA Today*, 1986

Kids are always chasing rainbows, but baseball is a world where you can catch them.

> **Johnny Vander Meer, former Cubs pitcher**
> *Time*, 1986

"When are you going to grow up, son?" they asked, knowing the answer. Never, not as long as baseball was being played, every day of every summer of every year. And here it is, eons later, and your hair is falling out, and you're still making your predictions and forgetting that you're in rush-hour traffic when you can flip on the radio and hear the game.

Bob Verdi
The Sporting News, 1986

As long as this game is taking, I'm going to have to shave again. One hour and twenty minutes to play three innings. Aw, come on, throw the ball!

Harry Caray
"Cubs Baseball," WGN-TV, Chicago, 1986

15. 1984: Near-Miracle

REGULAR SEASON

We've got a plan. Everything will be all right. Trust me.

Jim Frey, Cubs manager

These people are going wacko. Just get them a hit to give us a lead, and you get a standing ovation.

Keith Moreland, Cubs outfielder

Wrigley Field has become a baseball Fantasyland. A baseball game is an excuse for one big party, and things are happening here that don't happen anywhere else.

Bob Ryan
Boston Globe

I didn't get blamed when the Cubs lost. Why should I take credit for winning?

Yosh Kawano, Cubs equipment manager

You think I'm having fun? Fun to me is having a couple of beers and playing golf.

Jim Frey, in mid-August

I'm glad the Cubs are here. I always like to face up to things. . . . This is a Big-Time Face-Up.

Davey Johnson, Mets manager, facing the Cubs in mid-September

Both teams have improved so much. Just last year the big Mets series meant who finished last.

Jody Davis, Cubs catcher

A crucial series is one in which they put you in front of a firing squad if you lose.

Jim Frey, before the Mets series

The Mets left Chicago bloodied, beaten, and bowed.

Jerry Long, New York writer

Gentlemen, I think we've got a chance.

Jim Frey, leading by 8½ games with 12 left

All my life I've believed in miracles. . . . And now, after thirty-nine years of waiting, the miracle is happening. The Cubs are on their way to a National League pennant.

Ronald W. Reagan, speech, Economic Club of Chicago

Hey! Hey! Holy Cow! Cubs Clinch! Magic Number Reaches Zero; Sutcliffe a Hero.

Chicago Sun-Times, **headline**

My ship has come in. Good things come to those who wait . . . and wait . . . and wait.

Ernie Banks

We ain't trash no more, baby. Not for at least another thirty-nine years.

Ron Rapoport
Chicago Sun-Times

I was undressed in the clubhouse, drinking a cup of beer, when the game ended, and went back out to see the fans. I had to get me some of that.

Leon Durham, Cubs first baseman, on the curtain call on the final game of the regular season

George Orwell was right on the money; 1984 would be something special.

Ned Colletti, Cubs assistant director of public relations and publications

CHAMPIONSHIP SERIES

The Cubs in five games.

Jerome Holtzman
Chicago Tribune

We stand to lose something like $250,000 if the Cubs go all the way. That's just on future booking alone. We opened at 65–1 before the season started, and the betting didn't stop.

Jim Vacarro, Las Vegas sports book manager

I wouldn't care if they were played in Russia. It's a great feeling. It's neat. It's ice cream on the cake.

**Rick Sutcliffe, Cubs pitcher,
on the Series opening in Wrigley Field**

That baseball's poorest players are strutting about the national stage is a story of some significance. . . . In lotus land, where nothing is for real, the experience has turned into just another day at the beach. The only local color San Diego will provide is a bronze tan line.

Phil Hersh
Chicago Tribune

Because we have fairness, equity, truth, and justice and the American way on our side, we are going to slaughter those lousy wimps.

Mike Royko
Chicago Tribune

Let's face it, Mike. Chicago is a has-been slum of sausage eaters on the toxic waste Riviera of America. It's got a great past in the corruption department.

The San Diego Tribune, **editorial**

Well, if Chicago is a has-been slum of sausage eaters on the toxic waste Riviera, I guess the same can be said of Detroit. . . . We're both cities of shot and beer drinkers rather than wine sippers. We're still cities where you're more likely to find a guy with an eagle tattooed on his arm than a flower tattooed on his hip. And we're more likely to go to a tavern to pick a fight than to our backyard to pick an orange.

Mike Royko
Chicago Tribune

The truth is, San Diego is the sort of place where you have to drive forty miles to get Fritos. In this part of California, a trip to Marine World is considered a cultural excursion.

Steve Daley
Chicago Tribune

If the Cubs lost, all they had to look forward to was wearing galoshes and parkas and hats with flaps over their ears to ward off "The Hawk," the bitter Chicago wind, while they wait at snowswept streetcorners for buses that never arrive. Without that inner warmth, the glow that comes from knowing the Cubs had finally come home a winner, the wait could be unbearable.

Barry Gifford, Chicago-born writer

GAME ONE (CHICAGO): CUBS 13, PADRES 0

I asked Larry Bowa when the butterflies went away. He said after the first pitch.

Bob Dernier, Cubs centerfielder,
who hit the second pitch of the game for a home run

Five home runs, and I get a telegram telling me we didn't bunt enough.

Jim Frey, Cubs manager

I know one thing. I didn't have Chicago in a thirteen-run pool.

Dick Williams, Padres manager

All of a sudden it hit me. Those are the Cubs—the Chicago Cubs—beating the hell out of people that way. Bullies, that's what we've become. Big, bad, mean bullies. And, oh boy, does it feel great. Why didn't we think of this years ago?

Mike Royko
Chicago Tribune

In Game One of the National League Championship Series, their first postseason appearance since 1945, the Chicago Cubs trashed the San Diego Padres. Those poor Padres, the team unlucky enough to walk in on four generations of repentance.

Bill Plaschke
Seattle Post-Intelligencer

GAME TWO (CHICAGO): CUBS 4, PADRES 2

Intensity, a sporting word of the Eighties, surely wasn't born in Wrigley Field, but it definitely has found a home here.

Bob Verdi
Chicago Tribune

It's like we're in "The National League playoffs, starring the Chicago Cubs. Also with the San Diego Padres."

Tony Gwynn, Padres outfielder

Our players think they're playing Team USA.

Bob Brown, Padres announcer

Barring a minor miracle, and pending notification of next of kin, the San Diego Padres can be pronounced dead.

Fred Mitchell
Chicago Tribune

GAME THREE (SAN DIEGO): PADRES 7, CUBS 1

Hold That Champagne.

Chicago Tribune, **headline**

The Padres were simply enjoying a brief home-avocado advantage.

Bernie Lincicome
Chicago Tribune

The Cubs sort of overshadowed our season. It seems like everybody would like a replay of the 1945 World Series with the Cubs, and we'd like it, too.

Darrell Evans, Tigers first baseman

The pressure is on them now. There's just too much history of Cub failure.

Alan Wiggins, Padres infielder

GAME FOUR (SAN DIEGO): PADRES 7, CUBS 5

We'll use anybody we can to contain the White Sox. Well, I got the right city, anyway.

Dick Williams, Padres manager

It's gone! The Padres win! Oh, doctor!
Jerry Coleman, Padres broadcaster, on Garvey's
two-run game-winning homer in the bottom of the ninth

This was Frank Merriwell out of Alfred Hitchcock.
Barry Lorge, San Diego columnist,
on Steve Garvey's four-for-five, five RBI performance

One of the most dramatic LCS games ever played.
The Baseball Encyclopedia, Sixth Edition

When the ball started toward the fence, I froze in time.

Steve Garvey

The last person I saw do something like this was Roy Hobbs.

Tim Flannery, Padres infielder

Wonderboy, it wasn't. Just good, solid ash.

Steve Garvey

Garvey was so excited last night, he stopped at three ice cream parlors on the way home.

Dick Williams

I think our future senator picked up a few votes tonight.

Champ Summers, Padres infielder

GAME FIVE (SAN DIEGO): PADRES 6, CUBS 3

I'd feel more comfortable watching a war between the United States and Russia. This is too tense.

**Tom Lyons, Cubs fan,
at the Cubby Bear Lounge**

I went to the bathroom and it was 3–0. I came out and it was 6–3. I'm never going to the bathroom again.

**Sharon Streicher, Cubs fan,
at Murphy's Bleachers**

If Leon Durham could have sunk a tad further in his chair, he would have become a seat cushion.

**Fred Mitchell, on Durham's key error
in the seventh inning**
Chicago Tribune

The noise started when Rick Sutcliffe was warming up. . . .
The fans were making things happen. . . . I love the Cubs, and
I'm sure they'll deny it, but the fans intimidated them.

Ted Giannoulias, the San Diego Chicken

It was about the loudest I've ever heard a crowd. And it got
louder and louder. It started snowballing, and all of a sudden
they had momentum on their side. The next I knew, we were
on our way home.

Richie Hebner, Cubs outfielder

I don't know whether to get drunk, or not to drink. When this
is over, I want to check into an insane asylum for a few days.

Tim Flannery, Cubs infielder

The whole world is shocked right now. The whole world was
rooting for the Cubs.

Goose Gossage, Padres pitcher

Paradise Lost: Sutcliffe Fails to Stop Padres.

Chicago Tribune, **headline**

POST-MORTEM

They gotta be dying in Chicago today. It's like finding out the
day before Christmas that there will be no pennants.

Goose Gossage, Padres pitcher

I feel like there's been a death in the family.

James Thompson, Governor of Illinois

Today, the Cubs pennant hangs at half-staff.

> **Fred Mitchell**
> *Chicago Tribune*

Nobody died here. We'll bounce back.

> **Gary Matthews, Cubs outfielder**

Jack McKeon may be the MVP in all of this. In 1981, we had 3,600 fans on Fan Appreciation Day, and they booed the prizes.

> **Terry Kennedy, Padres catcher,**
> **on the Padres general manager**

I guess all the people across the country will have to cash in their Chicago Cubs caps now. But we don't need them. We don't need anybody but our fans. They're not too damn bad for surfers, are they?

> **Tim Flannery, Padres infielder**

It is all too evident now following the Padres stunning week-end effort against the miserable Chicago Cubs: San Diego is all grown up. A World Series city. No cops with attack dogs on the field—we prefer lifeguards with inner tubes—and we do just fine.

> **Nick Caneda**
> *The San Diego Tribune*

I know one thing. We took the '69 Cubs off the hook.

> **Terry Kennedy, Padres catcher**

It just happened again. And this time it was even worse. It's a monumental disaster. It makes 1969 seem like a minor aggravation.

> **Mike Royko**
> *Chicago Tribune*

You spend thirty years in this game, and you get good and damn disappointed. But this ranks the hell up there with any of them.

Dallas Green, Cubs general manager

The Cubs are losers. Again. And there is a sense of order to that, kind of like knowing that the Grand Canyon will always be an empty hole. Can you say forever?

Bernie Lincicome
Chicago Tribune

The Cubs had gotten beaten up for thirty-nine years, and now they picked a most untimely occasion to beat themselves.

Bob Verdi
Chicago Tribune

The Cubs, who were one game from winning their first pennant since 1945 . . . choked and blew the pennant to the San Diego Padres.

Davey Johnson, Mets manager

Choked? I look at what happened to the Cubs in San Diego this way. In Game Three in San Diego, we were overwhelmed by San Diego fans. I really believe it. In Game Four we were beaten, almost single-handedly, by Steve Garvey.

Jay Johnstone, former Cubs outfielder

They are going to the World Series, and we are going home. It is very hard to deal with. This will hurt for a long, long time.

Rick Sutcliffe, Cubs pitcher

Let's knock off the clown act for the rest of the country. Let's stop wearing futility like a badge. So it hurts. So the Cubs lost. So you got left at the altar one more time. So what? Lift your glass in salute, and have another. Opening Day is less than six months away.

Chicago Tribune

WORLD SERIES: TIGERS BEAT PADRES IN FIVE

The pitching matchups are a joke. What a bunch of nobodies the Padres pitchers are. Show, Thurmond, and Dravecky don't belong in the John Birch Society. They belong in the John Doe Society.

Mike Downey
Detroit Free Press

San Diego has no more chance of beating Detroit than a scarecrow has of dancing Swan Lake.

Bernie Lincicome
Chicago Tribune

Go get 'em cousins. And remember, there is more at stake than a mere baseball championship. Or even the honor of all the has-been slums or sausage-eating cities of America. We're counting on you to stop the spread of fern bars.

Mike Royko
Chicago Tribune

16. 1985: And Beyond

Everybody knows there have been bad winters in Cubs history before. Certainly, 1969 wasn't too hot. . . . But as bad winters in Cubs history go, this one was the all-time champ.

Bill Mazeroski's Baseball, **1985**

They've been playing ball in April for one hundred years, so I guess we'll have to try this year.

Jim Frey, Cubs manager, on the poor weather
Chicago Tribune, 1985

We're the National League champs. I'm sick of everybody saying Chicago this and Chicago that. That's a bunch of baloney, and we're going to dispel it.

Dick Williams, Padres manager
Sports Illustrated, 1985

That's what happens when you have a computer making up the schedule instead of humans.

Bobby Valentine, Mets coach, on not playing the Cubs until the middle of June, 1985

Makes me want to puke, just watching the way they win.

Whitey Herzog, Cardinals manager
Chicago Tribune, 1985

It looks like they mowed it with a helicopter.

Dave LaPoint, Giants pitcher, on the tall infield grass
Chicago Sun-Times, 1985

"What's the worst hitting team the Cubs can put on the field?" he asked. "You're looking at it," she said.

Bernie Lincicome
Chicago Tribune, 1985

Maybe the Cubs should have opened a booth at "Taste of Chicago" this weekend, so fans could stop by and sample a morsel of defeat.

Fred Mitchell
Chicago Tribune, 1985

No, I haven't slit my throat yet, but I may practice hanging myself.

> **Dallas Green, Cubs president, on the nine straight losses**
> *Chicago Sun-Times*, 1985

I worked part-time as an usher for the Washington Senators. If I could live through all those illustrious days, when a twelve-game losing streak was a quickie, then I think we can live through this.

> **Bob Ibach, Cubs public relations director**
> *USA Today*, 1985

It's not that the Cubs have been playing all that poorly while losing thirteen in a row, tying their club record. It's just that they have been playing like the Cubs. The real Cubs. Not the ones that put on that charade in 1984.

> **Tom Weir**
> *USA Today*, 1985

You bleepin' guys gotta be more creative. Ask me how it feels to lose! What can I say? When you lost twelve in a row, it feels horse manure. When you lose thirteen, it feels horse manure.

> **Jim Frey, Cubs manager**
> *Chicago Sun-Times*, 1985

When I managed softball teams and things were going bad, I'd have a party and get everybody drunk. . . . If I were Jim Frey and Dallas Green, I'd get the whole team together and get stiff as dead fish.

> **Mike Royko**
> *Chicago Tribune*, 1985

I was at Wrigley Field during the Cubs recent thirteen-game losing streak and I told manager Jim Frey I'd do anything to help. He looked at me and said, "Can you pitch?"

Tom Dreesen, comedian
The Hollywood Reporter, 1985

Sorenson, Sanderson, Fontenot, we don't know. . . .

Billy Connors, Cubs pitching coach, on his rotation
Chicago Sun-Times, 1985

This is like Custer's Last Stand, and they just got the last soldier.

Billy Connors, as Scott Sanderson fell and joined Sutcliffe, Eckersley, Trout, and Ruthven on the disabled list, 1985

I don't think a lot of people realize the mental burden I went through with the pitchers. I was catching five guys, and I didn't even know their names.

Jody Davis, Cubs catcher
The Sporting News, 1985

The Cub team picture could serve as a poster for the American Hospital Association.

Ron Rapoport
Chicago Sun-Times, 1985

Everybody in this game wants an opportunity. God knows, everybody on this team will get an opportunity.

Jim Frey, Cubs manager
Chicago Sun-Times, 1985

Geez, Dad. I saw the game today, and you stunk.
> **Matt Frazier, age five, to his dad George**
> *Chicago Tribune*, 1985

If George Washington's army had fought like Jim Frey's Cubs pitched yesterday, the Fourth of July would not be a national holiday.
> **Brian Hewitt**
> *Chicago Sun-Times*, 1985

I saw his eyes light up real wide when he saw it. I closed mine, and he opened his wide.
> **Steve Trout, on a home-run pitch to Steve Garvey**
> *Chicago Sun-Times*, 1985

I said throw the bleeping ball over the plate and get some bleeping outs. That's what I said. What the bleep are you gonna walk a team that's gonna steal three hundred bases?
> **Jim Frey, after his team walked ten Cardinals**
> *The Scoreboard News*, 1985

There's been more noise in my father's graveyard than there's been in Wrigley Field the last few days.
> **Richie Hebner, Cubs infielder**
> *Chicago Sun-Times*, 1985

It's much easier to have a little more enthusiasm when you're in first place than in fifth place, but our players have to realize they put themselves in fifth place.
> **John Vukovich, Cubs coach**
> *The Scoreboard News*, 1985

Those ivy-busting grizzlies of last year have become the Care Bears of '85. Talk about tame.

New York Post, 1985

The cry now is to let the Cubs play night games in Wrigley Field if they wish. Just don't bother installing lights.

Bob Verdi
The Sporting News, 1985

I had a dream the Cubs and the White Sox met in the World Series this year. Both of them lost.

Fred Holstein, Cubs fan
Chicago Sun-Times, 1985

That's the prediction here, a one-two-three finish at the wire with the Cubs in front, the Mets and Cards only slightly behind. Not more than five games will separate the three teams.

Jack Lang (the Cubs finished thirty-seven games behind the Mets)
New York Daily News, 1986

Whether they win the East or not, the Cubs will be better than last year.

Allen Barra and George Ignatin
Inside Sports, 1986

If everyone stays healthy, the Cubs should challenge for the division championship.

Rick Hummel
The Sporting News, 1986

I think the Cubs will come back to where they were before, maybe not to the point of '84, but close.

Pat Gillick, Blue Jays general manager
Sport, 1986

You've seen this movie before. Same plot, same ending. Not much action.

Fred Mitchell, as the Dodgers shut out the Cubs
Chicago Tribune, 1986

Tuesday, it will be back to business . . . the Cubs to Atlanta, where they should hold the mayo and the losses.

Bob Verdi, as Rick Sutcliffe had food poisoning
Chicago Tribune, 1986

Am I, a lifelong fan of the Chicago Cubs, destined to spend the next four months watching them grovel around the cellar floor with the hated Cardinals, bitter? You bet. I have been bitter since 1969, when the New Yorkers took a glorified semi-pro team . . . to the world championship, permanently disfiguring the distinction of that particular appellation.

John McGrath
Los Angeles Times, 1986

I told Jimmy [Frey] that if we played .500 ball, it would be a good year, we should go to church. . . . I figured we had no chance.

Don Zimmer, former Cubs coach
Chicago Tribune, 1986

I don't think God could have come down and made this team win.

Don Zimmer
The Oregonian, 1986

The Dallas Green-built Cubs are a bad ballclub that had an exceptional year in 1984 and has since sunk back to the level at which it belongs.

> **Peter Pascarelli**
> *Philadelphia Inquirer*, 1986

If we sweep them in all eighteen games, we'll be back in there.

> **Steve Stone, as the Cubs were 17½ games**
> **behind the Mets**
> "Cubs Baseball," WGN-TV, Chicago, 1986

The Cubs, it's rough. The fans are ordering food to go.

> **Billy Crystal, comic**
> "Baseball: An Inside Look," NBC-TV, 1986

Reporter: Have you been unlucky, ineffective, or terrible in earlier outings?
Eckersley: All of the above.

> **Dennis Eckersley, Cubs pitcher**
> *Chicago Tribune*, 1986

I'd rather be lucky than good.

> **Ed Lynch, Cubs pitcher, catching a line drive**
> **to start a triple play, 1986**

17. Brains and Flakes

I missed my first train because the porter said it was a Pullman, and I didn't know what a Pullman was and wasn't going to take a chance on finding out.

> **Guy "The Busher" Bush, pitcher,**
> **coming to the Cubs in 1924**

In my first season as a pro, a runner was stealing, and I swear my throw hit the centerfield fence on the first bounce. My manager came up to me: "Kid, in this league they slide, they don't fly."

Gabby Hartnett, Cubs catcher

I don't think I'm old enough to play golf. I'm used to other people chasing balls I've hit. Damned if I'm going to run after a little ball myself.

Rogers Hornsby, Cubs player/manager

I thought he meant a real farm and go to work. So I went down to my aunt and uncle's farm at Lockhart, Texas, and went to work.

Rogers Hornsby, when told as a rookie that he was to be "farmed out"

Listen, who are you gonna believe, a record book or ol' Bobo?

Bobo Newsom, Cubs pitcher, when a sportswriter disputed his wins in the Pacific Coast League, 1932

I can't play in Wrigley, because the left field line isn't straight like it is in other parks. It's crooked.

Lou Novikoff, Cubs outfielder

Hazlewood: You're pitching today; what do you want me to do with the mound?
Bithorn: Well, you might move it ten feet closer to home plate.

Hi Bithorn, Cubs pitcher, to Cubs groundskeeper Harry Hazlewood

I never tried to outsmart nobody. It was easier to outdummy them.

Dizzy Dean, Cubs pitcher

It puzzles me how they know what corners are good for filling stations. Just how did these fellows know there was gas and oil under here?

Dizzy Dean

My parents had six kids before me, and my dad didn't get to name any of them until me. When I came along he tried to catch up.

Cal McLish, Cubs pitcher, on his given name of
Calvin Coolidge Julius Caesar Tuskahoma McLish

You know, Willie, somebody should take a picture of us together. We're the best two players in the league. You with your bat and your speed and me with my great arm and brains.

Clyde McCullough, to Willie Mays, 1953

Zick: Hi, I'm Zick.
Hack: I haven't been feeling so well myself.

Stan Hack, Cubs manager,
upon first meeting Cubs pitcher Bob Zick, 1954

Drop the anchor. We're going to fish this spot until I catch the biggest fish in this lake wearing my sunglasses.

Ernie Banks, Cubs shortstop,
after dropping his sunglasses in the lake, 1959

When I fish I can think about things . . . such as how some of those pitchers got me out. While I wait for some fish to bite, I figure out how some of those pitchers got me on the hook.

Billy Williams, Cubs outfielder

I love fishing. I've always loved it. I started in the sewers of Brooklyn, and worked my way all the way to Lake Michigan. Imagine.

Joe Pepitone, Cubs first baseman, 1972

The damn war was over. It seems the Japs had quit about fifteen days after we left the States. I guess they heard old Hig had beat the Germans and was coming after them.

Kirby Higbe
The High Hard One, 1967

During the fight, I swung at five guys and missed every one of them.

Rick Monday, future Cubs outfielder, 1970

Baseball was my favorite sport. I was too chicken to play football.

Burt Hooten, Cubs pitcher

Most Cub fans didn't do too well in school. If they had, they would have been Yankee or Reds fans.

Rick Schwab
Stuck on the Cubs, 1977

Baseball really improved my mind. Not even Commissioner Kuhn could outsmart me. I ran a trail of lighter fluid all the way to his foot, lit that beauty, and he must've jumped four or six feet. Yowww! What a scream he let out. He never figured out who did it.

Moe Drabowsky, former Cubs pitcher, 1982

My greatest prank was staying around as long as I did.

Moe Drabowsky, 1982

To me, the clubhouse was a place to put my uniform on and take it off. Sitting around in my underwear in front of twenty-five other men equally well-attired was not the greatest part of my career.

**Steve Stone, Cubs broadcaster
and former Cubs pitcher, 1983**

I'd like to come back as a utility infielder, or a Triple Crown-winning horse. I could either sit on the bench for twenty years and draw a tremendous pension, or spend the rest of my life as a stud.

Dee Fondy, former Cubs first baseman
The Sporting News, 1983

Caray: Mike Marshall is going back to Los Angeles to get cocaine for his injured foot.
Stone: Harry, that's Novocaine.

Steve Stone and Harry Caray
"Cubs Baseball," WGN-TV, Chicago, 1984

Don't worry, that cat ain't gonna get nobody out.

**Billy Connors, Cubs pitching coach,
after a fan threw a black cat on the field at Shea, 1984**

She keeps saying, "Cubs win! Cubs win!"

**John Felske, Phillies manager, renting Billy Connors'
house in Florida, on Connors' parrot, Lucy, 1984**

The words that come out of her mouth will make you blush. I think I know where she learned them, though.

Billy Connors, on Lucy
Chicago Tribune, 1984

He's up for Digger of the Month. He's eight bodies ahead of last year. He's already had a couple of hat tricks.

**Richie Hebner, Cubs infielder,
on his father, a cemetery worker, 1985**

We knew one of us would be a professional ballplayer. I was the dumb one with the strong arm. I knew it would be me.

Steve Trout, one of ten children
Chicago Tribune, 1985

Talk about disappointments. One of the biggest disappointments of my twenty-two year pro baseball career is that somebody stole my Star Patrol helmet.

Jay Johnstone
Temporary Insanity, 1985

How will I be remembered? Maybe someday a rookie will hear my name mentioned and say: "Jay Johnstone? He was so crazy that when he came into the hotel room, his pillow jumped out of the window." And that kid might have a chance in this game.

Jay Johnstone
Temporary Insanity, 1985

I damaged some houses. But I'd like to see those guys on the Tour try to hit a slider.

Leon Durham, on his first round of golf
The Sporting News, 1985

Retirement was upon me. . . . There was golf, but I knew golf wasn't the same when you played every day without having to sneak out of the office to get to the first tee.

Jack Brickhouse
Thanks For Listening, 1986

I was one of the youngest players in the major leagues and certainly the most naive. . . . There was the day I spent hours trying to find the key to the batter's box.

Thad Bosley, Cubs outfielder, 1986

We've only played one-fourth of the season. We know things can turn around in a hurry. Things turned around in a hurry for us last year, but they turned the wrong way.

Jim Frey, Cubs manager
The Oregonian, 1986

We've got to understand that we're talking about an exhibition game here. It's not like we're fighting for the Chicago River. The winner doesn't get the Sears building.

Jim Frey, on a Cubs/White Sox game
Chicago Tribune, 1986

A lot of people around the National League have already conceded the MVP to Gary Carter, but I think Ron Cey's got a legitimate shot. No doubt he'll be a candidate for MVP: Most Valuable Penguin.

Steve Stone
"Cubs Baseball," WGN-TV, Chicago, 1986

18. Wrigley Field

When the flags are blowing in, pitch to the flags. When the flags are blowing out, don't pitch.

Bob Buhl, Cubs pitcher

People remember their days at Wrigley Field. It's the same there; it never changes. And when you leave . . . you're still there.

Ernie Banks

I always wanted to bring a pennant to Wrigley Field. It's the one big disappointment in my life.

Ernie Banks, upon retirement, 1972

You no have to be home-run hitter to hit home runs here.

José Cardenal, Cubs outfielder

Every player should spend a year with the Cubs to have fun in Wrigley Field.

Alvin Dark, Cubs infielder

Cubs fans are long-suffering, then again not-so-long suffering. They have Wrigley Field.

Bill Veeck

I hate those magic carpets. The ball bounces around like a Yo-Yo. . . . Just give me grass, daylight ball, and another pennant flying over Wrigley Field.

Bill Nicholson, former Cubs outfielder

To water that grass in beautiful Wrigley Field would be a dream come true.

Rick Bosetti, Phillies outfielder,
who wants to urinate on every major-league field, 1976

First thing the day of a game, even before a good Cub fan relieves himself, he checks the wind. . . . When the wind blows out at Wrigley Field, the Cubs win. The wind is to the Cubs what spinach is to Popeye.

Rick Schwab
Stuck on the Cubs, 1977

Wrigley Field is a Peter Pan of a ball park. It has never grown up and it has never grown old. Let the world race on—they'll still be playing day baseball in the friendly confines of Wrigley Field, outfielders will still leap up against the vines, and the Cubs . . . well, it's the season of hope.

E. M. Swift
Sports Illustrated

Baseball is a game of exquisite moves, of subtlety no less demanding than that of a concert orchestra. It is a thrilling sight to watch the pitching motion of Steve Carlton, the swing of Billy Williams or Rod Carew. . . . Beauty is where you find it. You can even find it at Wrigley Field.

Jim Langford
The Game Is Never Over, 1980

When the snow melts away
Do the Cubbies still play
In their ivy-covered burial ground?
Steve Goodman
"A Dying Cub Fan's Last Request," 1981

If the Cubs lose two more games, Jane Byrne will move into Wrigley Field.

Harry Caray, when the mayor took an apartment in a crime-ridden neighborhood to boost morale, 1981

"Wrigley Field," said Leo, a Cub fan since the 1940s, "is the only place where you can watch a game and get eaten alive at the same time. The Wrigleys furnish everything you need. The game, the stadium, even the bugs."

David Bush
San Francisco Chronicle, 1981

The obvious occurred to me: That a ballpark is, first of all, a park. Looking over the outfield fences I saw a city neighborhood, but there, inside the boundaries, was parkland so beautifully tended and tranquil that it was almost jarring. No wonder so many people make a habit of going to baseball games even when their team is not doing particularly well.

Bob Greene
Chicago Tribune, 1981

When we were kids, we used to go to the circus all the time—only we called it Wrigley Field.

Tom Dreesen, comedian
"The Tonight Show," NBC-TV, 1981

If we all go to Chicago and play the ultimate baseball game in the sunshine of Wrigley Field, we will be able to be home by five, have a small barbecue, eat tofu-burgers, and live in a perpetual state of grace.

Bill Lee
The Wrong Stuff, 1984

Even if you hear that your heroes
Scored fourteen runs and still
Lost by two, stand by them.
No one promised you a rose garden;
Settle for ivy-covered bricks.

Jim Langford
The Cub Fan's Guide to Life, 1984

Wrigley Field is more than just a ballpark. It is a landmark, an urban icon, and a demonstration of what big cities are supposed to be all about. It could not exist in the suburbs any more than Rush Street could exist in Danville.

Paul Gapp, architecture critic
Chicago Tribune, 1984

You see the old bleachers and the old scoreboard, built in 1937. There's not a discordant note in the appearance of this park.

Bill Veeck
Sports Illustrated, 1984

The bleachers . . . where the scent of suntan oil, broiled hot dogs, and spilled beer create a wondrous feeling of euphoria —a feeling that neither crowds, hard benches, long ticket lines, nor the endless trek to distant toilets can diminish. The bleachers aren't just concrete and steel, cheap seats, and concession stands; they're a state of mind, a way of life, the best of summer.

Bill Veeck
Chicago Magazine, 1984

My loyalties are with the ballpark. I equate my youth with the ballpark and, in Wrigley Field, you never grow up.

Jerry Pritikin, Chicago advertising executive
Chicago Sun-Times, 1985

Chicago is an old-fashioned, traditional American city, with subways and buses and neighborhoods with bungalows. The Cubs and Wrigley Field represent something to hang on to.

Mike Royko
Esquire, 1985

The unrestrained joy of Ernie Banks forever will remain at Wrigley Field, which forever will be called "friendly Wrigley Field."

Art Spander
San Francisco Examiner, 1985

Baseball indoors, on carpeting, is a crime against nature. I'll close my eyes and imagine that I'm back in the bleachers, warmed by the sun and cooled by the stiff lakeshore breeze, squinting in the sunlight to look across the field of real grass, past the ivy-covered low brick walls along the first- and third-base lines, to home plate.

Jan Even, editorial columnist, former Chicagoan
Seattle Times, 1985

No escalators, sure, and the fans aren't exactly always good neighbors, but if you had to see one last game before dying, you'd want day baseball in this graying but priceless heirloom.

***Sport*, 1985**

Wrigley Field is the world's biggest day-care center.

Phil Hersh
Inside Sports, 1985

It [his winter home] is so isolated, Wrigley Field could burn down, and nobody could contact me with the news.

Dallas Green, Cubs president
The Sporting News, 1985

That's wishful thinking, Dallas.

Bill Conlin
The Sporting News, 1985

What a beautiful ballyard. . . . I wouldn't be surprised if they're standing at attention *in* their apartments, too, during the Anthem and the stretch. The neighborhood is part of the game, and the game is part of the neighborhood.

Keith Hernandez
If at First, 1986

Face it, this is a Cub town and has been for more than a half a century, not because the Cubs have had the better or worse teams but because of Wrigley Field, which is an absolute treasure.

Jerome Holtzman
Chicago Tribune, 1986

2008. Baseballs will be orange, bats will be made of zinc, scoreboards will be powered by plutonium, and Wrigley Field will be the only park in the majors without nuclear power.

Mike Downey
The Sporting News, 1986

19. Lights Out

High-class baseball cannot be played at night under artificial light. The benefits derived by patrons attending a baseball game are largely due to fresh air and sunshine. Night air and electric lights are a poor substitute.

**Clark Griffith, Senators owner
and former Cubs pitcher, 1930**

I felt the game should be played in daylight.

**Philip K. Wrigley, Cubs owner,
on why he didn't install lights**

It isn't a whim. It's a matter of public responsibility. . . . How can anybody sleep with a loudspeaker going, thousands of people hollering, and cars being parked all over their yards? All you'd need is some louse like me to put in lights, and it would wreck things.

Philip K. Wrigley

By the time a player gets home after a night game, the dog is asleep. There is no relationship.

Ernie Banks, Cubs infielder

Baseball was meant to be a daylight game, but we're going to continue to have night baseball as long as people want to make money.

Rogers Hornsby
My War with Baseball, 1962

That heat, day after day, drains your energy. By August, the regulars were tired, but Leo [Durocher] kept us in there without an occasional day off. When the Mets made their move, we had nothing left.

**Don Kessinger, former Cubs shortstop,
on why the team blew the 1969 pennant**

Don't listen to that stuff about playing all day games wearing you out. I loved it. That's just a poor excuse. The players just couldn't cut it and they had to blame it on somebody.

**Peanuts Lowrey, 1940s Cubs outfielder,
on the 1969 Cubs**

Having all day games at home is one of the best things about playing for the Cubs.

Ron Santo, Cubs third baseman

The greatest game in the world is Wrigley Field in Chicago because there you have afternoon baseball. The game was made to be played in the daytime.

Shag Crawford, umpire

The effect of the sun's rays is an intangible factor. . . . The Cubs could play their home games at seven in the morning (but what a downer to see Jack Brickhouse right after you wake up).

Rick Schwab
Stuck on the Cubs, 1977

Decker: And on the seventh day, the Lord rested and came to beautiful Wrigley Field and watched the Chicago Cubs play His own game on His own green grass under His own lights.

Organic Theatre Company
Bleacher Bums, 1977

I don't wanta hear that old stuff about day ball killing the Cubs again. The Cubs killed the Cubs.

Lynn McGlothen, Cubs pitcher, 1979

Give me a doubleheader funeral in Wrigley Field
On a sunny weekend day (no lights).

Steve Goodman
"A Dying Cub Fan's Last Request," 1981

I hope those fellows down there are aware that there are no lights in this ballpark.

Hank Greenwald, on a slow-moving game at Wrigley
"Giants Baseball," KNBR-Radio, San Francisco, 1981

Show me a Chicago Cub without sacks under his eyes, and I'll
show you a Cub who's only been with the team two weeks.
Bill Caudill, Cubs pitcher, on the hardship of day games
Sports Illustrated, 1982

They can play night ball, but not in our neighborhood.
**Charlotte Newfield, member of Citizens United for
Baseball in Sunshine (C.U.B.S.), 1982**

Noise pollution at Wrigley can't be that much of a problem.
There's nothing there to cheer about.
Rep. John F. Dunn, Illinois legislator, arguing for lights
The Sporting News, 1982

You need a special kind of player at Wrigley Field—one who
likes to get to sleep before midnight.
Steve Stone, Cubs broadcaster, 1983

I can't shed any light on that.
**Stanton Cook, president of the Tribune Company,
on Dallas Green's comment that Wrigley
would have lights, 1983**

Ban the installation of lights at Chicago's Wrigley Field. If
Cubs General Manager Dallas Green wants to begin a new
tradition in the toddling town, he can start by fielding a win-
ning team.
Fred Guzman
San Jose Mercury News, 1983

There will be no lights in Wrigley Field as long as I'm with the
club.
**Jim Finks, Cubs president,
later replaced by Dallas Green, 1984**

The whole subject bores me.

> Jim Frey, Cubs manager
> *Sport*, 1984

When baseball and TV signed the contract didn't they know the Cubs were in baseball and this might happen? Did they just find out in the last week that we're in the league?

> **Jim Frey, when the playoff dates were changed, 1984**

Some players don't like to get up at eight in the morning to get ready for a day game. Me, I'd like to play day baseball regularly. That way, I'd be able to go home, have dinner and watch a ballgame on TV every night.

> **Pete Rose, Reds player/manager, 1984**

For a family man, day baseball is perfect. . . . Of course, when I pitch, I prefer to pitch at night.

> **Rick Sutcliffe, Cubs pitcher**
> *Sport*, 1984

What a story the Chicago Cubs are! A little ballpark where they play day baseball will draw two million people this year. That's like drawing four million in Yankee Stadium!

> **Harry Caray, Cubs broadcaster**
> *Sports Illustrated*, 1984

The main difference between day and night baseball is that if you want to go out for a beer after a day game, it's still Happy Hour.

> **Gary Matthews**
> *Sport*, 1984

It feels so good—when you're home,
Let's hear it for the sunshine boys,
You can't do no wrong.

On the road they beat 'em night or day,
When they're at home they play the natural way.
C'mon Cubbies hey hey hey hey,
Roll all day long.

> **Henry Farag**
> "The Land of Wrigley," 1984
> Performed by Stormy Weather

I liked day ball. I treated it as a job. Got up early, ate, went to the ballpark. Game ended, went home, had a dinner with my family, went to bed at a reasonable hour. Night people, they're the ones who can't handle it. Guys with talent, I've seen them lose it on Rush Street.

> **Billy Williams**
> *Baseball Digest*, 1985

Frey: Any other questions? Nobody here's asked me about the lights today. Ask me about the lights.
Reporter: What about the lights?
Frey: No comment.

> **Jim Frey**
> *The New Yorker*, 1985

C'mon. Get this game away from television and out in the open where it belongs, before we all turn around and find out nobody plays the game in the daytime anymore but Bosco and Gumby and Alfalfa—standing in the outfield at Wrigley, watching the tumbleweeds roll by.

> **Ernie "Bob" Kielbasa**
> *San Francisco Examiner*, 1985

Baseball, which is a great American sport, is really conceived to be played in daytime. When they first got their hot dog, the sunshine and their baseball, they weren't thinking of artificial lights. I don't think they were thinking of it as a way to disrupt a community, and I don't think, for certain, they need to put lights in this community.

Jane Byrne, former Chicago mayor
The Sporting News, 1985

You're out, O-U-T. The Cubs are out. Justice is a southpaw, and the Cubs just don't hit lefties.

Judge Richard Curry, Circuit Court, Cook County, upholding the constitutionality of noise pollution laws aimed at prohibiting night baseball in Wrigley Field, 1985

Do those who schedule playtime
For the games of our national pastime
Have the right to interfere with bedtime
By starting the game at nighttime
Instead of the customary daytime?

Judge Richard Curry, 1985

It's not just a question of lights in Wrigley Field. It's a question of *if* Wrigley Field. If Wrigley Field, in my opinion, doesn't have lights . . . at some time in the future, it won't be a field in some time in the future.

Commissioner Peter Ueberroth, speech, National Press Club, Washington, D.C., 1985

I think there are a lot of people out there who consider Dallas Green and Peter Ueberroth a couple of lousy ogres who want to destroy Wrigley Field. Nothing could be further from the truth.

Dallas Green, still preferring lights
Chicago Tribune, 1985

The Commissioner wants the [World Series] games played in a National League East division park. St. Louis and Pittsburgh are the closest to Chicago.

John Madigan, Tribune Company vice-president
USA Today, 1985

It [the Commissioner's suggestion] is unpatriotic. . . . It borders on treason, and I will recommend he be tried.

Mike Royko
Chicago Tribune, 1985

As far as the Cubs are concerned, I want to make it clear that we have not—as part of our agreement—required them to play at night.

Jim Spence, senior vice-president, ABC-TV, disputing
Commissioner Ueberroth's reading of the
TV contract, 1985

I've got a solution. The White Sox will win the American League pennant, and we'll play all seven World Series games at Comiskey Park.

Gary Matthews, Cubs outfielder
Chicago Sun-Times, 1985

If it comes to that [playing at Comiskey Park], I'd rather see them play before a studio audience under the Michigan Avenue bridge, or better yet, on the backlot at WGN.

Jerome Holtzman
Chicago Tribune, 1985

We're getting absolutely no cooperation from the community at all. We have to look at all the alternatives.

Dallas Green, Cubs president
Chicago Sun-Times, 1985

What are they going to say next—give us lights, or we'll blow up Wrigley Field? It's domestic terrorism.
Nancy Kaszak, C.U.B.S. president
Chicago Sun-Times, 1985

The last time anybody checked the standings, however, the Cubs were three games under .500, fourteen games out in fourth place, and if Wrigley Field did have lights, they'd be out.
Steve Wulf
Sports Illustrated, 1985

Day games don't feel like real games. It's like spring training. It's like they don't count.
Dwight Gooden, Mets pitcher
The Oregonian, 1986

If Dante were alive, he'd reserve the last circle in hell for anyone who tries to put lights in Wrigley Field.
Sebastian Dangerfield
Sport, 1986

By NL fiat, the Cubs would play their postseason games in the dreaded Busch Memorial Stadium. . . . What we have here is a daylight mugging by the owners, amply aided and abetted by none other than Cubs President Dallas Green, who sounds as if he is loving every minute of a ploy aimed at the installation of lights at the shrine at Addison and Clark.
Bill Conlin
The Sporting News, 1986

I don't like it a bit. Who is the National League to come in here and tell us where our team should play? The thing that bothers me is we accept it. Who is the league? Do you know them? You can't spell the name of the guy who runs it. I can't. What is this all about? This is a city. We are people. We have rights.

Harold Washington, mayor of Chicago, 1986

It was Mr. Cub himself, Ernie Banks, who would stand outside the dugout on a warm afternoon at Wrigley Field and announce, "It's a great day to play two." The team's current management is of the opinion no day game is that great. Perhaps the quality of Chicago weather has declined in the fifteen years since Banks retired.

Joe Gergen
The Sporting News, 1986

Asking the Cubs to play their postseason games at St. Louis' Busch Stadium is like asking Scarlett O'Hara to sell her property to condo developers.

Mike Downey
Los Angeles Times, 1986

Why are the Chicago Cubs worried about playing the home playoff games in St. Louis? What do they think this is, the NBA or the NHL, where everybody makes the playoffs?

Jonathan Witt, letter
The Sporting News, 1986

The whole brouhaha is moot, of course. The sad-sack Cubs have as much chance to win a pennant as Chernobyl has to be the site of the next International Boy Scout Jamboree.

Bill Conlin
The Sporting News, 1986

If the Cubs did turn this season around and win the division, I'd bet enough Cubbies would show up with flashlights to keep the team in Wrigley where it belongs.
Steve Duin
The Oregonian, 1986

20. Managers, Coaches, and Scouts

Only parents who have one child, which possesses four grandparents and twenty or thirty aunts all trying to spoil it, can understand in full the difficulties of the manager's job.
Johnny Evers
Baseball in the Big Leagues, 1910

Suggest I stop in Springfield, Illinois, en route to check out Abraham Lincoln.
Jack Doyle, Cubs scout, when sent to Illinois to check out George Vernon Washington

My gum company made a $40 million profit last year, and I can't get the financial writers to say a word about it. But I fire a manager and everybody shows up.
Philip K. Wrigley, Cubs owner

This is something every batting coach has to do, pretend he's teaching pitchers how to bunt. That's how he gets paid.
Jim Brosnan
The Long Season, 1962

This coach had Joe Goddard on his team. . . . In high school he was the best hitter in the state. But the coach batted him eighth in the lineup! I said, "Why do you have Joe Goddard battin' eighth, good of a hitter as he is?" He said, "Because he's a catcher, and catchers always bat eighth."

Frank DeMoss, Cubs scout, 1981

I think they recycle more managers than cans.

Billy North, former Cubs outfielder
San Francisco Chronicle, 1981

Baseball to me was just like punching a clock. I had to take orders from all kinds of dumb guys.

Ernie Broglio, former Cubs pitcher,
on managers and coaches, 1983

I have one son who even knows the names of first-base coaches. That is like knowing the name of the secretary of commerce.

George Will
Newsweek, 1985

Losing a third-base coach is like losing a sock in the dryer.

Bernie Lincicome, on the departure of Don Zimmer
Chicago Tribune, 1986

I like teaching. The tough part is finding someone who will listen to you.

Davey Lopes, Cubs infielder, on coaching
The Sporting News, 1986

Joey Amalfitano Manager 1979-1981

That didn't bother me. I was once cheered by 92,000 people in Los Angeles when I made an error and the Dodgers won.

Joey Amalfitano, on getting booed at Wrigley for pulling starter Bill Caudill, 1981

Cap Anson Manager "Pop" Hall of Fame 1879-1897

As an umpire baiter, Cap made Leo Durocher look like a Boy Scout.

Eddie Gold and Art Ahrens
The Golden Era Cubs, 1985

Everywhere Cap goes, the argument goes.

Harvey Frommer
Baseball's Greatest Managers, 1985

Ernie Banks Coach Hall of Fame 1972-1973

I like my players to be married and in debt. That's the way you motivate them.

Ernie Banks
New York Times, 1976

Lou Boudreau Manager Hall of Fame 1960

To the bewilderment of baseball, Wrigley cut a deal with WGN Radio, the Cubs flagship station, and sent manager Charlie Grimm to the broadcast booth for announcer Lou Boudreau. It was an even trade—both sides lost.

Bruce Nash and Allan Zullo
The Baseball Hall of Shame 2, 1986

I don't remember how many games we lost that season, but they can't fault my strategy. Nobody ever listened to it.

                    Lou Boudreau, who won 54 and lost 83 in 1960

Frank Chance   Manager   "The Peerless Leader"
Hall of Fame   1905–1912

After a game lost this season Chance yelled at his men, "You're a fine lot of curs, you are." Not exactly the sort of talk boys expect from their father. Rumor has it that "curs" was not the word used, but it will do under the circumstances.

                    New York Evening Mail, 1908

You do things my way or you meet me after the game.

                    Frank Chance

He was called the "Peerless Leader," also "Husk," for his fine physique which included a pair of fists that were always ready to augment his point of view.

                    Donald Honig
                    Baseball's 10 Greatest Teams, 1982

College of Coaches   Six Managers   1961–1965

I believe that managers are expendable. In fact, I believe there should be relief managers, just like relief pitchers, so you can keep rotating them.

                    Philip K. Wrigley, Cubs owner, 1959

We certainly cannot do much worse trying a new system than we have done for many years under the old.

                    Philip K. Wrigley, on his revolving managers, 1961

The College of Coaches concept is the best thing that has happened to baseball since the spitball.
Elvin Tappe, Cubs manager, 1961

It's different, all right. Instead of getting into one doghouse, you can get into ten.
Don Zimmer, Cubs infielder, 1981

We have tried both ex-Cub players and ex-Cub managers. It just doesn't seem to work. The best protection we can give our managers is to advise them to get out of baseball.
Philip K. Wrigley, abandoning the concept, 1965

It was terrible. Every two weeks a different coach. One day you're stealing bases, the next day you're hitting home runs.
Ron Santo, former Cubs infielder
Sports Illustrated, 1984

The College of Coaches approach—if they [the children] are really causing you problems, get relatives, in-laws, etc., to take turns managing them. This will keep them confused right up to their twenty-first birthday. Then you can put them on waivers.
Jim Langford
The Cub Fan's Guide to Life, 1984

Billy Connors   Coach   1982–1986

Maybe it's only coincidence, but Rick Sutcliffe and Dennis Eckersley became dominant pitchers immediately after joining the Cubs from the American League. He also helped Steve Trout, once frustrated by unfulfilled potential, become a winner. All right, so he teaches the spitball.
Steve Wulf
Sports Illustrated, 1985

Leo Durocher   Manager   "The Lip"   1966–1972

I've seen him on the spot many a time—but I've never yet failed to see him got off the spot.

> **Tom Meany**
> *Sport*, 1947

Whether Leo operates at cards, at baseball, at life, a hustle is built in. With time a man does best to cease moralizing and stand back in admiration of all that gall and glitter.

> **Roger Kahn**
> *How the Weather Was*, 1973

I had always felt that Leo would play a convicted rapist if he could turn the double play.

> **Jim Bouton**
> *I Managed Good, But Boy Did They Play Bad*, 1973

Leo was Leo, and there is no one else quite like him in sports. One day you hate him, the next you love him. You never trust him.

> **Howard Cosell**
> *Cosell*, 1973

Call me anything, call me motherfucker, but don't call me Durocher. A Durocher is the lowest form of living matter.

> **Harry Wendelstedt, umpire, 1974**

When Leo touched his nose, it meant the hit-and-run was on. But there was a problem. The son-of-a-gun was always picking his nose.

> **Herman Franks, former Durocher coach**

Leo would get all spiffed up, dressed to kill, spending all his money, while his mother was working at the Netherlands Plaza Hotel, scrubbing floors. Son, he would hold the lamp while his mother was cutting wood.

Happy Chandler, former commissioner

As a manager, he made a science out of dirty play, and his most effective weapon was the beanball.

Peter Golenbock
Bums, 1984

Then you had Leo Durocher, who only thought he knew it all.

Augie Donatelli, former umpire
The Sporting News, 1986

Lee Elia   Manager   "Banty Rooster"   1982–1983

Lord knows I've always felt the most beautiful thing in this game is the roar of the crowd.

Lee Elia
Chicago Tribune, 1985

Charlie Fox   Manager   "Irish"   1983

Some organizations know how to win . . . and some don't: The Chicago Cubs replaced manager Lee Elia with Charlie Fox, whose mind is still replaying the 1942 season.

Glenn Dickey
San Francisco Chronicle, 1983

Charlie Fox, who once punctuated a point he was making to Montreal Expos righthander Steve Rogers with a right to the jaw.

Bill Conlin
The Sporting News, 1986

Herman Franks   Manager   1977–1979

In recent years, if nothing else, we've had clean livers for managers. Whitey Lockman, Jim Marshall, and Herman Franks
are all men you'd bring home for dinner (except with Herman
you'd lock the refrigerator door).

Rick Schwab
Stuck on the Cubs, 1977

Jim Frey   Manager   1984–1986

If it's true that we learn by our mistakes, then Jim Frey will be
the best manager ever.

Ron Luciano, broadcaster
San Francisco Examiner, 1981

Has the emotional intensity of a comatose eggplant.

Bill James
Sport, 1982

I'm with the media now, and we need you for an interview
outside. We'd appreciate it if you didn't chew tobacco or pick
your nose.

Earl Weaver, to Frey
Chicago Tribune, 1984

It is very difficult to disagree with Frey on any aspect of hitting since he may know more about hitting than anyone who
never did much of it himself.

Bernie Lincicome
Chicago Tribune, 1985

Cubs manager Jim Frey, a minor-league batting champion of 1957, used to soak his bats in motor oil, an appropriate balm for one whose travels led him practically everywhere but to the major leagues.

> Tom Callahan
> *Time,* 1985

I'll tell you what a challenge is. A challenge is being too short to play, not being able to see real well and wanting to play in the big leagues. I know all about challenges.

> **Jim Frey, taking over the Cubs, 1984**

I gave 'em fourteen years of mediocrity.

> **Jim Frey, on his playing career**
> *Chicago Magazine,* 1984

You know, it's like sending your daughter to college. One day she's eighteen, and she's going away and she's still a girl. Then, the next day, she comes home, and she's a woman and she's gorgeous.

> **Jim Frey, on the transformation of the Cubs**
> *Chicago Magazine,* 1984

Managing is a job where you lose four straight games in August and you lie awake all night tryin' to think what the blank to do and you get up without knowin' the answer. Then you come into the clubhouse smiling and clappin' your hands, and you say, "All *right!* Everybody relax! We've got 'em now!"

> **Jim Frey**
> *The New Yorker,* 1985

I always imagined that Chicago would be so grateful to the next man to bring the Cubs a championship that he would be given a statue in a public place, a pension for life and have, if not a street, at least a pizza named after him.

Bernie Lincicome, on Frey's firing
Chicago Tribune, 1986

Frankie Frisch   Manager   "The Fordham Flash"
Hall of Fame   1949–1951

Baseball is like this. Have one good year, and you can fool them for five more, because for five more years they expect you to have another good one.

Frankie Frisch

Preston Gomez   Manager   1980

If I had known then what I know now, I never would have taken this job.

Preston Gomez, 1980

Charlie Grimm   Manager   "Jolly Cholly"
1932–1938, 1944–1949, 1960

With his Chicago Cubs down by nine runs, manager Charlie Grimm, coaching at third base, dug a hole and buried his lineup card.

Dan Schlossberg
The Baseball Catalog, 1980

It was a different world then, and a lot more fun, especially with Charlie Grimm around.

Bill Veeck, lounging in the bleachers, 1984

Cubs scout: Spotted a pitcher who stopped a team cold for nine innings. One ball hit out of the infield and that was a foul fly.

Grimm: Forget the pitcher. Send the guy who hit the foul.

Charlie Grimm, 1948

These hands were never made to carry a briefcase.

Charlie Grimm, 1949

Stan Hack   Manager   "Smiling Stan"   1954–1956

It's so small we don't even have a town drunk. Everyone has to take a turn.

**Stan Hack, on his hometown
of Grand Detour, Illinois**

Gabby Hartnett   Manager   Hall of Fame   1938–1940

If you don't want anybody to talk to the Big Guy, Judge, *you* tell him.

**Gabby Hartnett, when Commissioner Landis saw a
photograph showing Hartnett talking to Al Capone, 1938**

Rogers Hornsby   Manager   "The Rajah"
Hall of Fame   1930–1932

You might not have liked what was on his mind, but you always damned well knew what it was.

Burleigh Grimes, former Cubs pitcher

He was a very cold man. He would stare at you with the coldest eyes I ever saw. We never knew what the hell he was thinking.

Billy Herman, former Cubs infielder

As I remember, he was selfish, a strange guy who couldn't manage a quarter's worth.

                                                              Ty Cobb, 1960

It might be said that if a rattlesnake bit Hornsby, the snake would die. He was blunt, hard-boiled, stubborn, tactless, opinionated. . . . As a manager, he spent more time in hot water than all the lobsters in Maine.

                                              Irv Haag, sportswriter, 1974

Unfortunately, his only interest besides baseball was an evidently unhealthy one in himself. His greatest dislikes were futility and anything less than an all-out effort—crimes of which he naturally enough never found himself guilty.

                                                              Jim Enright
                                                        Chicago Cubs, 1975

He endeared himself to no one.

                                                           Donald Honig
                                                    Baseball America, 1985

If players thought I was mean, they should have spent a little time under John McGraw. . . . When a writer asked "Are you married?" the rookie answered, "You'd better ask Mr. McGraw."

                                                         Rogers Hornsby
                                                My War with Baseball, 1962

Whitey Lockman   Manager   1972–1974

The Cubs took on the image of their manager. It was the blond leading the bland.

                                                  Eddie Gold and Art Ahrens
                                                     The New Era Cubs, 1985

Joe McCarthy   Manager   "Marse Joe"
Hall of Fame   1926–1930

I hated his guts, but there never was a better manager.

Joe Page, former pitcher

They tell me we don't look very good on paper. Well, we don't play on paper.

Joe McCarthy, new Cubs manager, 1926

Listen, any manager who can't get along with a .400 hitter ought to have his head examined.

Joe McCarthy, asked about Ted Williams
Sport, 1973

A manager needs just about three things. A good memory, patience, and being able to recognize ability . . . and not only to recognize it, but to know what to do with it.

Joe McCarthy, 1977

Rabbit Maranville   Manager   Hall of Fame   1925

Rabbit Maranville (whose "leadership" generally led the team into speakeasies). . . .

Eddie Gold and Art Ahrens
The Golden Era Cubs, 1985

Never take a backward step out there. The first backward step a little man takes is the one that's going to kill him.

Rabbit Maranville

Jim Marshall   Manager   1974–1976

There's been a vacuum in Chicago radio talk programming since Leo's lip departed the airwaves. Whitey Lockman and Jim Marshall, the managers who followed Durocher, were as exciting as career civil service workers closing in on their pensions.

> **Rick Schwab**
> *Stuck on the Cubs,* 1977

Gene Michael   Manager   "Stick"   1986–

Gene Michael . . . comes to us with the ringing endorsement of George Steinbrenner, the Yankee visionary who twice found Michael unfit to manage his baseball team. Would you buy a used manager from that man?

> **Bernie Lincicome**
> *Chicago Tribune,* 1986

Reporter: Tell me, Mr. Michael, are you aging in Chicago?
Michael: Oh, no. I got my gray hair from the curveball.

> **Gene Michael, lifetime .229 hitter**
> *Chicago Tribune,* 1986

Billy Williams   Coach   Hall of Fame 1980–1982, 1986–

The good hitters hit the hanging curve, the bad hitters miss it. . . . There's only about twenty or thirty hits a year difference between a bad hitter and a good one, you know. You hit those thirty hangers, and you'll see your name up there in the papers.

> **Billy Williams**
> *The New Yorker,* 1981

Don Zimmer   Coach   1984–1986

The designated gerbil.

> **Bill Lee, Red Sox pitcher**
> *Newsweek*, 1978

Zimmer's a pistol, a short, gnarly guy who's never drawn a check outside of baseball and is proud of it.

> **Johnny Bench**
> *Catch You Later*, 1979

Zimmer's face looks like a blocked kick.

> **Joe Garagiola**
> "NBC Game of the Week," NBC-TV, 1980

Pee Wee Reese: To my buddy: I finally made it! Eat your heart out! P.S. Not even pinstripes can make this body look good.

> **Don Zimmer, coaching the Yankees, in a letter to Reese**
> *The Sporting News*, 1983

I want to make sure nobody's in my uniform.

> **Don Zimmer, on why he arrived at the park early**

When I was a manager, what I looked for in a third base coach was someone who drank a little beer and bet a little on the horses.

> **Don Zimmer, third base coach**
> *Sports Illustrated*, 1984

I'll tell you when you know you're really in trouble. . . . It's when your traveling secretary that you've had fun with, and this writer that you've had fun with and people that you talk to in the front office . . . all of a sudden, they don't want to look at you. . . . And you can smell the rat.

> **Don Zimmer, near his firing**
> *Chicago Tribune,* 1986

21. Owners, Executives, and Employees

Chicago Tribune   Owner   1981–

The Chicago Cubs were sold the other day to the *Chicago Tribune.* That's a great move for the Cubs, and for the people of Chicago, to be able to buy a paper on street corners from Cub players. If you're going to stay with the organization, why not go all the way?

> **Bob Uecker**
> "The Tonight Show," NBC-TV, 1981

Any company that can invest in the Chicago Cubs has a view of the future we cannot even begin to comprehend.

> **Jeff MacNelly, political cartoonist**
> *The Sporting News,* 1982

The Tribune people would like to tear down "old" Wrigley Field. The truth is that Wrigley Field has been renovated so many times it is younger than the Tribune Tower. They should be worrying about removing that monstrosity from Michigan Avenue as a service to the city's progress and leave the ballpark alone.

> **Bill Veeck**
> *Chicago Sun-Times,* 1985

Marla Collins Ballgirl 1982–1986

There *is* entertainment value in my being in shorts on the field, and I can't say that if I weighed three hundred pounds it would be quite the same thing.

> **Marla Collins, in her nude pictorial**
> *Playboy*, 1986

That's the best thing I've seen out of uniform all year.

> **Harry Caray, Cubs broadcaster, 1986**

At the risk of sounding ungallant, this has to be said: Marla Collins looks better with her clothes on.

> **Bernie Lincicome**
> *Chicago Tribune*, 1986

Cub tradition is the issue. In the long history of this team, nobody playing for the Cubs ever appeared nude in public. The only possible exception was an old-time first baseman who was suspected of being a flasher.

> **Mike Royko**
> *Chicago Tribune*, 1986

Marla Collins may no longer be the Cubs ballgirl, but fans will now be able to see more of her than ever.

> **George Boyd, Chicago, letter**
> *Chicago Tribune*, 1986

Jim Finks President 1983–1984

Stand tall when the bullets are flying, take the heat, and stay on course.

> **Jim Finks, his philosophy**

Dallas Green   General Manager 1981–   President 1984–

He has moved his family to Winnetka, where I'm confident he will become an ideal citizen, providing, of course, he doesn't put up lights in his backyard.

Jerome Holtzman
Chicago Tribune, 1982

Green wants to build a Cub-a-Dome, with a plastic roof, plastic grass, plastic ballplayers, and plastic ushers telling the plastic fans that booing is not permitted.

Mike Royko
Chicago Sun-Times, 1982

I'm not going to second-guess Dallas Green. All I'm going to say is that Dallas Green traded his best pitcher for a sack of garbage.

**Whitey Herzog, Cardinals manager, on the trade which
sent Mike Krukow to the Phillies for Dickie Noles,
Dan Larson, and Keith Moreland, 1982**

He's big, he's good-lucking, he's tough, he doesn't take no bullshit from no one. When he walks down in that dressing room it looks like John Wayne to me.

Tom Dreesen, comedian, 1985

Pity the poor athlete who suns instead of runs during spring training drills, thinking that Dallas Green is locked in his office, only to discover that baseball's version of Idi Amin is glaring from some shadowy perch in the grandstands.

Bob Verdi
Chicago Tribune, 1985

He possesses the look and sound, the fury and bluster of an enraged tenor. . . . At six feet five and 250 pounds, he fills rooms with his presence—that carriage, that voice—but, most of all, with his unbridled, explosive ego.

Bill Brashler
Chicago Magazine, 1985

If Dallas has one drawback, it is that his voice has acoustics that belong in Carnegie Hall.

Ned Colletti
You Gotta Have Heart, 1985

"Humility" is not a word he has spent time studying. And that's good.

Bill Veeck
Chicago Magazine, 1985

Ticket sales, fun at the old ballpark—none of that is Green's bottom line. Winning is. He gagged on the "lovable losers" image that was such a part of Cub lore. . . . True Cub fans, meanwhile, had grown proud of the label "long-suffering." No wonder they don't understand the guy.

Dan McGrath
San Francisco Chronicle, 1986

When you came to Chicago, you'd look in the Cubs dugout and you just knew you had a shot at 'em every time. You knew they'd find some way to figure out how to lose.

Dallas Green, Phillies pitcher, early 1960s
Sports Illustrated, 1984

William A. Hulbert   Owner   1876–1882

William A. Hulbert was a typical Chicago man. He never spoke of what *he* would do, or what *his club* would do, but it was always what *Chicago* would do.

Albert G. Spalding
America's National Game, 1911

Bob Kennedy   General Manager   1977–1981

Bob Kennedy was a good guy. One of the hardest things for him as Cub general manager was to avoid saying what he really thought of Dave Kingman. Kingman was the only Cub who could hit the ball out of the infield then, except for Bill Buckner.

Brian Hewitt, *Chicago Sun-Times* sportswriter

Andy Lotshaw   Trainer   1921–1952

Andy became a trainer by practice. . . . He took some correspondence courses, interviewed people and practiced bandaging on his wife Laura until sometimes she looked like an Egyptian mummy.

Bill Veeck, 1985

Turpentine, lemon oil, olive oil, and some other things I ain't tellin'.

Andy Lotshaw, on the ingredients in his famous body rub

Wid Matthews   General Manager   1950–1956

If what you did yesterday still looks big to you, you haven't done much today.

Wid Matthews, his slogan

The Cubs break your heart one day and have you wondering whether they'll ever win another game. And the next day they look so wonderful they have you floating in the clouds.

Wid Matthews, 1950

Charles Murphy   Owner/President   1905–1913

Charles Murphy . . . has no sentiment for baseball, only for the money there may be in it for him. In fact, the "Chubby One" is considered a joke all over the National League, and nowhere more so than in Chicago. He is out for the "dough," and nothing else about the great sport appeals to him.

Sam Crane
New York Evening Journal, 1908

Albert G. Spalding   President 1882–1892
Owner 1882–1902   Hall of Fame

Every wholesome American boy knows everything worth knowing about baseball—the famous players, the historic contests, and the notable features of the sport.

Albert G. Spalding, 1884

The future of baseball is without limit. The time is coming when there will be great amphitheaters throughout the United States in which citizens shall be able to see the teams take part in the finest athletic struggles of the world.

Albert G. Spalding
Sporting Life, 1908

Bill Veeck   Employee/Executive/Bleacher Bum
1933–1986

Somehow we will just have to muddle through opening day
without him. And we will have to adjust to a few sad facts:
The gross national consumption of beer has diminished, some
say measurably. Every day now, one good book goes unread.
And marches against handguns and for peace and civil rights
have one fewer peg leg pounding the pavement.

Bill Brashler
Chicago Magazine, 1986

Hell, the Old Hustler has been dead so often I've lost track. I
know I'll find him again, if only I go to Miller's Pub just before
noon some day next week. I'll order two beers and he'll stump
along, plop into the booth, and insist on paying for that round
and the next six.

Ray Sons
Chicago Sun-Times, 1986

I never met another man like Bill Veeck. He could be out-
spent and out-foolished and, occasionally, out-maneuvered.
But you could not out-think him or out-drink him and certainly you couldn't do both at once.

Rick Talley
Cubs Vine Line, 1986

Bill Veeck, though not a player, left us a happy monument,
one that he sculpted as he saw fit. He made an art of his life.

***Minneapolis Review of Baseball,* 1986**

Bill Veeck, a valued man with values . . . belongs in the Hall of Fame down here. As for where he's headed, we can only caution the folks up there to be ready. Nobody will be getting much sleep anymore.

Bob Verdi
The Sporting News, 1986

I worked for Bill five years. I should say I worked *with* Bill five years. Anyway, I figure I really worked with him for ten years, because I only slept half as much as I normally would have.

Roland Hemond, former White Sox general manager
The Sporting News, 1986

I built those bleachers. . . . Management was never in those bleachers. I'm a tiny voice. I don't mean anything. More and more, we're being led. We're being manipulated. Somebody has to say it's wrong, and I believe it to be wrong.

Bill Veeck, when the Cubs decided to sell advance tickets to bleacher seats, 1985

Bill Walker   President   1933–1934

Bill Walker will start on the mound today for the Cardinals. This Bill Walker isn't to be confused with the Cubs' Bill Walker, who is confused enough as it is.

Warren Brown
Chicago Herald-Examiner, 1934

I lost count of how many times Bill Walker fired me in the 1934 season, but I guess all I'd have to do to find out is to look up how many games we lost.

Charlie Grimm
Jolly Cholly's Story, 1968

Philip K. Wrigley   Owner 1932–1977
President 1934–1977

If the Phillies can't win, I'm pulling for the Cubs because of just one man—Phil Wrigley. He's one pioneer who puts baseball ahead of everything—his team, his hopes. If something isn't good for the complete game, you'll never sell it to him.

Bob Carpenter, Phillies owner, 1969

He only has two speeches. The short one, "Thank you," and the long one, "Thank you very much." I like the long one.

Mrs. Philip K. Wrigley
Sports Illustrated, 1971

What makes the Cubs so outstanding? A man named Mr. Phil Wrigley. . . . He is kind, considerate, helpful, understanding and loyal, and Wrigley never thinks of the Cubs alone. It's baseball, and then the Cubs.

Ernie Banks
Mr. Cub, 1971

I tested all kinds of chewing gum to spark my sputum. I heard a lot of fellows swear by Beechnut, I leaned to Wrigley's Spearmint myself. Maybe I kind of had a soft spot for Wrigley's because of Mr. Wrigley owning the Chicago Cubs. I always got a little extra kick out of using his gum to help beat his baseball team.

Gaylord Perry
Me and the Spitter, 1974

Money grubbers, in their chase to the bottom line, may mock Wrigley as an eccentric. Fans of success may scoff at the Cubs as hopeless losers. Chicago knows better.

Jim Enright
Chicago Cubs, 1975

Wrigley is just dandy in Doublemint, but he should have a guardian with him when he starts making decisions in baseball.

Harold Parrott
The Lords of Baseball, 1976

If all the owners had been as fair to the players as Mr. Wrigley was, we wouldn't need a Players' Association.

Randy Hundley, Cubs catcher, 1977

I knew I was in trouble when I went to negotiate my contract and Mr. Wrigley's advisor had to ask me what position I played.

Barry Foote, Cubs catcher
San Francisco Chronicle, 1982

Philip Knight Wrigley knew more about things and less about people than anyone I've ever met. Baseball is a game of people. So no one was more unequipped to deal with it than he was.

Bill Veeck
Inside Sports, 1982

I became President because I got all the blame anyway.

Philip K. Wrigley

It's a thankless, discouraging job trying to run a ballclub.

Philip K. Wrigley, 1953

William Wrigley, Jr.   Owner   1915–1932

Wrigley, the chewing gum millionaire, was blessed with an inventive mind and no need to hew to baseball's hidebound traditions. Unfortunately, he knew very little about the sport.

Ray Sons
Chicago Sun-Times, 1985

The Wrigleys had been such haphazard, uninterested, and underfinanced owners (or, less euphemistically, dumb, dumb, and dumb) that competing against them was like pulling the wings off dead flies.

> **Phil Hersh**
> *Inside Sports*, 1985

22. Philosophy

I'd rather disappoint a president of the United States than disappoint a kid.

> **Gabby Hartnett, Cubs catcher, 1930**

When you are in the big leagues, wear good suits, good shoes, white shirts, and smoke good cigars.

> **Gabby Hartnett, 1946**

It ain't bragging if you can back it up.

> **Dizzy Dean, Cubs pitcher**

I think anything you try to do to change anything, even if you explain it to them, the majority of people object.

> **Philip K. Wrigley, Cubs owner**

A man feels pressure only when he doesn't know what he is doing.

> **Gene Mauch, Cubs infielder**

The only way to prove that you're a good sport is to lose.

> **Ernie Banks, Cubs infielder**

Reporter: How come you seem to have so many enemies in baseball?
Hornsby: Wouldn't want them phonies for friends, anyway.

Rogers Hornsby, former Cubs manager
New York Times, 1962

Whenever you think you've got something really great, add ten percent more.

Bill Veeck
The Hustler's Handbook, 1965

My friends have been with me all the way. All a friend can do, or anybody can do, is give you a chance. The rest is up to you.

Kirby Higbe
The High Hard One, 1967

A person doesn't have to smile. It's what comes out of the heart that means something.

Billy Williams
Billy: The Classic Hitter, 1974

If you're in professional sports, buddy, and you don't care whether you win or lose, you are going to finish last. Because that's where those guys finish, they finish last.

Leo Durocher
Nice Guys Finish Last, 1975

Charlie Grimm was a nice guy, and he helped the Cubs finish first five times. And then Leo Durocher finished last in 1966.

Jim Langford
The Cub Fan's Guide to Life, 1984

If there is one thing I firmly believe it is that everything happens for the best.

> **Leo Durocher**
> *Nice Guys Finish Last,* 1975

It's well-known most ballplayers are a bunch of asses.

> **Bill Madlock, former Cubs infielder, 1979**

The worst mistake you can make is making the same mistake twice.

> **Dallas Green, Cubs general manager, 1981**

I haven't read the front page of a newspaper in thirty years. Too many killings and stuff like that.

> **Chuck Tanner, former Cubs outfielder**
> *Inside Sports,* 1981

Every time you learn something, it helps you—maybe a week, a month, maybe a year from now. Once you stop learning— let me tell you—you're going to be in the second row looking at somebody else playing.

> **Ferguson Jenkins, Cubs pitcher, 1983**

I'm a fan of escape. I happen to think escape is a very good thing.

> **Bill Veeck**
> *Washington Post,* 1984

You make your own bounces.

> **Keith Moreland, Cubs outfielder**
> *Seattle Post-Intelligencer,* 1984

The big possum walks late.

Harry Caray, Cubs broadcaster

Momentum is overrated.

Jim Frey, Cubs manager, 1984

I'm not much of a chemistry guy, you know. Chemistry to me is a pinch-hit double with the bases loaded.

Jim Frey
Chicago Tribune, 1985

If we can send a man to the moon, why can't we cure the 1-2-3 inning?

Jerome Holtzman
Chicago Tribune, 1985

A friend of mine once told me the words *fall* and *fail* look a lot alike but they don't mean the same thing. I might fall, but I'm not going to fail.

Rick Sutcliffe, Cubs pitcher
Chicago Sun-Times, 1985

You can always take a shot to improve yourself. . . . If you can better yourself by one inch you should take it.

Dallas Green, Cubs president
Chicago Magazine, 1985

No high-fives until the late innings. Play to win, but play clean. Say what you mean, but pick your spots. Put personal problems aside when you play the game. Respect and friendship are the keys.

Gary Matthews
They Call Me Sarge, 1985

Some days the best you can do isn't very good.

> **Gary Matthews**
> *They Call Me Sarge*, 1985

My high school coach, Roosevelt Johnson, taught me an important lesson. He told me, "No one can make you feel inferior, without first getting your permission."

> **Lou Brock, speech,**
> **at his Hall of Fame induction, 1985**

If you're gonna wait for luck or fate in this life, you're gonna be disappointed. There's only two times in the year when you get gifts—at Christmas and on your birthday. The rest of the time you make your own breaks.

> **Ron Cey, Cubs infielder**
> *Cubs Vine Line*, 1986

23. Wild Times

What are you running here? A Sunday school or a baseball club?

> **King Kelly, White Stockings infielder, when**
> **owner Albert G. Spalding asked about his bad habits**

I have to offer only one amendment. In that place where the detective reports me as taking a lemonade at 3 A.M., he's off. It was straight whiskey; I never drank a lemonade at that hour in my life.

> **King Kelly, when Spalding had detectives**
> **follow certain players, 1885**

It depends on the length of the game.
>   **King Kelly, on an English tour,**
>   **when asked if he drank during the game**

Our men this year do not drink, and they take pride in keep-ing up the reputation of the club. . . . We shall no longer endure the criticism of respectable people because of drunk-enness in the Chicago nine.
>   **Albert G. Spalding, White Stockings owner**
>   Chicago *Daily Baseball Gazette*, 1887

Captain A. C. Anson desires me to announce, in black type, at the head of this column, that the Chicago baseball club is com-posed of a bunch of drunkards and loafers who are throwing him down.
>   **Hugh S. Fullerton**
>   *Chicago Inter-Ocean*, 1897

Yeah, I learned something: If you drink whiskey, you won't get worms.
>   **Hack Wilson, Cubs outfielder, when manager**
>   **Joe McCarthy dropped a worm in a**
>   **whiskey bottle to show him something**

Hack Wilson usually played in the outfield, but I'd put him at first base because he wouldn't have as far to stagger to the dugout.
>   **Mike Royko**
>   *Chicago Sun-Times*, 1981

Everyone Shoots Par at Gabby's Bar.
>   **Gabby Hartnett, former Cubs catcher,**
>   **sign at his bar, 1947**

Gabby was my manager at Jersey City. . . . After every game, there were two cases of beer in the clubhouse—one case for Gabby and one case for the players.

Joe Stephenson, Red Sox scout

If, after winning a game, one of my players wants a night on the town, all he has to do is call me up—I'll go with him.

Leo Durocher, Cubs manager, 1966

A major-league coach I used to know as a player told me, "Hig, these guys that play today are so tight that they will go into a bar looking for a good-looking girl and sip on one beer half the night."

Kirby Higbe
The High Hard One, 1967

I'm the only guy besides Ruth who was ever suspended by the Yankees. Babe Ruth and me.

Joe Pepitone, Cubs outfielder

Booze, broads, and bullshit. If you got all that, what else do you need?

Harry Caray
Playboy, 1976

Caray . . . popped his first six-pack with Abner Doubleday.

Ray Sons
Chicago Sun-Times, 1985

Reporter: What's your handicap?
Noles: Most days, those two six-packs.

Dickie Noles, Cubs pitcher
Inside Sports, 1982

I don't even drink whiskey. If it had been a cold beer, it might have been a different story.

> **Gary Matthews, Cubs outfielder,**
> **when a fan at Shea threw a whiskey bottle, 1984**

You ask yourself what happens if you fail, how you could duplicate the kind of salary you're making in baseball. The answer is you couldn't. And once you start dwelling on that, you might be tempted to use something to get you through the night.

> **Bill Madlock, former Cub, on drugs and alcohol**
> *The Sporting News*, 1984

They strolled into the courthouse in $500 three-piece suits, $150 custom-made shirts, $200 shoes by Gucci, and a quarter's worth of character. It was the week of the "rat fink," baseball style. Attendance was by special invitation of the United States Attorney.

> **Bill Veeck, on the Pittsburgh drug trials**
> *The Sporting News*, 1985

From a baseball fan: "Of course Commissioner Peter Ueberroth wants to investigate drugs—he heard Harry Caray sing."

> **Irv Kupcinet**
> *Chicago Sun-Times*, 1985

To some people, this is beer. To me, it's bread and butter.

> **Harry Caray, Cubs fan and Bud man**
> *Chicago Sun-Times*, 1985

I'm a Cub fan, but not a Bud man, since I think it tastes like swill.

> **Don Pitt, Chicago, letter**
> *Chicago Tribune*, 1986

I see a lot more old drunks than old doctors.
Harry Caray
"Cubs Baseball," WGN-TV, Chicago, 1986

Am I through with Rolling Rock for life? There's a chance I may resume beer when the season starts. Since when isn't a manager allowed to change his mind?
Jim Frey
Chicago Tribune, 1985

In the old days we'd get a guy a bottle and tell him to get lost.
Jim Frey, on Ryne Sandberg's slump
Chicago Tribune, 1985

I didn't smoke, drink or do drugs, and believe me, this job can drive you to it.
Davey Lopes, Cubs infielder, on his trim physique
Sports Illustrated, 1985

Welcome to the Bad News Bees. This is the last refuge of retired drug abusers.
Ken Reitz, admitted amphetamine junkie with the Cubs, on the Single-A San Jose Bees, 1986

You play well on uppers for a while, but it catches up to you. . . . You think you're playing well, but you're playing like shit.
Ken Reitz
San Francisco Chronicle, 1986

Caray: Put it on my tab.
Stone: A sizable tab, no doubt.
Steve Stone and Harry Caray
"Cubs Baseball," WGN-TV, Chicago, 1986

I thought about not working the game because I felt so terrible. But then I thought that Harry must feel this way every day after his nights on the town.

> **Steve Stone, ill with food poisoning**
> *Chicago Tribune,* 1986

24. Women, Wives, and Family

I guess Miss Looker and I can wait. She's as anxious to have the Cubs win as I am.

> **Solly Hofman, Cubs infielder, when told**
> **to delay his wedding until after the season, 1908**

That's the only way the poor girl will ever get anything from that bum of a husband.

> **Frank Chance, Cubs manager, fining a player**
> **$2,500 and giving it to his wife**

The people pay money to see me at my best, not tired or hung over. I go out with girls—I'm human—but I figure if I don't get the pitch I want between seven P.M. and midnight, forget it. I'll always get another chance to go to bat.

> **Rogers Hornsby, Cubs infielder**

I always told that kid if he kept going up in those things he'd come down in one the hard way someday.

> **Rogers Hornsby, upon hearing of the**
> **death of his son in a plane crash**

They all know what to do. The problem is trying to make it interesting.

Jack Brickhouse, Cubs broadcaster, on Liz Taylor's husbands during their honeymoons

I spray my tobacco shots and brown streams flow down my chin. It almost cost me my marriage. Once I was trying to show off in front of my wife, and I spat on her open-toed shoes. She wouldn't speak to me for weeks.

Steve Hamilton, Cubs pitcher, 1972

Next trip, the Cubs ought to bring the wives and leave the players at home.

Billy Valentine, former umpire, on a poor road trip, 1973

All I remember about my wedding day is that the Cubs dropped a doubleheader.

George Will
The Pursuit of Happiness and Other Sobering Thoughts, 1978

I do that [kiss his bat] when I need something. It's like your wife—when you want something from her, you butter her up.

Cliff Johnson, Cubs first baseman
Sports Illustrated, 1980

No honeymoon is complete without a visit to Cooperstown, a picturesque hamlet that by coincidence is where baseball's Hall of Fame is located. Audre was ecstatic.

Eddie Gold, *Chicago Sun-Times* sportswriter
Inside Sports, 1981

Jerry Koosman is one of the class guys in our game. And he has a great wife, if there is such a thing as a great wife.

Ralph Kiner, former Cubs outfielder
The Sporting News, 1982

That's when I knew my career was really in jeopardy.

Allen Ripley, Cubs pitcher,
after his wife hit four of his five pitches, 1982

I'd rather my wife wasn't here, and she knows it. I've got to worry about where to take her to dinner. If she wasn't here, I could go to dinner anytime I wanted. Then I could come back, lay in bed smoking a cigar and drinking a beer and watch the Kansas City game on television.

Jim Frey, Cubs manager, on road trips
Chicago Tribune, 1984

When I left home for Evansville, my father said one thing: "Don't embarrass your mother."

Jim Frey
Chicago Tribune, 1984

A lot of women say they would like to be men. Of course, we die ten years sooner. I think we die sooner because we give a shit whether the Cubs win or lose.

Tom Dreesen, comedian, 1985

My wife's been trying to get me to do the twist for thirty-five years.

Don Zimmer, Cubs coach
Chicago Sun-Times, 1985

I don't talk to the enemy anymore. . . . I don't have anything to say to the hitters. They are the ones who keep my old lady from going to the mall.

Lee Smith, Cubs pitcher
Chicago Tribune, 1985

I got advice from everybody—all my friends in the neighborhood. Everybody was saying, "Don't do it."

Gary Matthews, on his first marriage
They Call Me Sarge, 1985

You always remember the first hit. The first marriage. The first divorce.

Gary Matthews
Chicago Tribune, 1985

Must be my mom's cooking—nothing against my wife, of course.

Jody Davis, Cubs catcher, on why he hits well in Atlanta
Chicago Sun-Times, 1985

Being a relief pitcher is a lousy job, plain and simple. You pitch two shutout innings, and they're roaring. Today you give up two runs, and they're booing. It's like your wife's cooking. Good one night, lousy the next.

George Frazier
Chicago Tribune, 1985

I would never ignore a woman.

Harry Caray
"Cubs Baseball," WGN-TV, Chicago, 1986

Harry likes pretty young things.
> **Marla Collins, Cubs ballgirl**
> *Playboy*, 1986

I'm pretty much like a lot of girls. My main things are jewelry, furs and cars . . . mink coats, sports cars and leather, not to mention diamonds.
> **Marla Collins**
> *Playboy*, 1986

I'm really proud of you, Lee Arthur. Your earned-run average keeps going higher and higher.
> **Lee Smith's mother, watching her pitcher son**
> *The Sporting News*, 1986

25. Hitting and Missing

You can talk till the silver moon gets a copper lining about the beauties of scientific ball and the pretty features of two to one games, but if the crowd gets a chance to express itself, it will rise up and yell for games where home runs skip down the lea and two-baggers rake their way amid sylvan lanes. There is something enchanting about the music of a long, hard drive.
> **W. A. Phelon**
> *Chicago Journal*, 1908

Are you trying to insult Hubbell—coming up here with a bat?
> **Gabby Hartnett, Cubs catcher, to Lefty Gomez**
> **at the All-Star Game, 1934**

You all done? You comfortable? Well, send for the grounds-keeper and get a shovel because that's where they're going to bury you.

> **Dizzy Dean, Cubs pitcher,**
> **to a hitter who dug in**

You have a round ball and a round bat, and you try to hit it square.

> **Hank Sauer, Cubs pitcher**

The Cubs didn't have fights in my days. If one did take a swing, he'd have missed.

> **Jim Brosnan, former Cubs pitcher,**
> **on the late 1950s**

I can spit farther than he can hit a ball.

> **Rogers Hornsby, Cubs hitting instructor,**
> **to a father who brought his son for a tryout, 1960**

I wanted to know my bat a little better.

> **Richie Ashburn, Cubs outfielder, on why**
> **he slept with his bat during a slump**

When you have a lifetime average of .358 you don't have any slumps.

> **Rogers Hornsby, former Cubs infielder**
> *New York Times,* 1962

You know what Rogers Hornsby told me forty-five years ago? It was the best batting advice I ever got, "Get a good ball to hit!"

> **Ted Williams**
> *The New Yorker,* 1984

Reporter: Are you a hot-weather hitter, Billy?
Williams: I hope so. It's the only kind of weather I got right
now.

**Billy Williams, Cubs outfielder,
playing in Houston, 1963**

The hits I had were accidental, really. I tried everything. I
was a righthander but I tried batting lefthanded for a while.
That didn't work. The only thing I didn't try was an ironing
board.

**Bob Buhl, Cubs pitcher, on his major-league record
of eighty-eight straight hitless at-bats, 1961–1963**

My folks are touring Italy, visiting their folks. By the time
they get word of my grand slam, I'll probably be back on the
bench.

Joey Amalfitano, Cubs second baseman, 1964

I think my hitting is progressing. It's becoming progressively
worse.

Hank Aguirre, Cubs pitcher, lifetime .085 hitter

I finally came to see that baseball, no matter how much I loved
the game, was not life and death. All you can do is the best
you can. You can go oh-for-thirty, and you're still living.

Ron Santo, Cubs infielder, 1972

There are only five things you can do in baseball—run, throw,
catch, hit, and hit with power.

Leo Durocher
Time, 1973

Slumps are mostly a mental thing, I'd say. And it always seems that when you're not goin' good, that's the day you're facing a Gibson or a Seaver.

Billy Williams
Billy: The Classic Hitter, 1974

I've always been given credit for the line, "Home run hitters drive Cadillacs, singles hitters drive Fords." Well, I never said it, although it was said about me, by [pitcher] Fritz Ostermueller.

Ralph Kiner, former Cubs outfielder, 1976

I'd rather hit home runs. You don't have to run as hard.

Dave Kingman, Cubs outfielder

Stealing is an option. Hitting is a necessity.

Lou Brock
Sports Illustrated, 1979

Bill Buckner had a nineteen-game hitting streak going and always wore the same underwear. Of course, he didn't have any friends.

Lenny Randle, White Sox infielder, 1980

Today all the clubs chart hitters—they know where to pitch to them, how to get them out. A lot of parks are bigger, and the pitchers are bigger, too—and they're *good*. Hitting never seems to get easier.

Jim Frey
The New Yorker, 1981

What's one home run? If you hit one, they are just going to want you to hit two.

> **Mick Kelleher, former Cubs infielder,**
> **homerless in ten years, 1981**

What the Cubs need is a little fat guy who can hit the ball out of the park.

> **Mike Royko**
> *Chicago Sun-Times,* 1981

He's afraid of the ball. If he ever gets a real knock-down pitch, he'll shit all over home plate.

> **Gordon Goldsberry, Cubs scout,**
> **on a young prospect**

That's what batters write Santa Claus for—a sled and a high curve ball.

> **Joe Garagiola, former Cubs catcher**
> "World Series," NBC-TV, 1982

What the (censored) is my opinion of his performance? (Censored), he beat us with (censored) three (censored) home runs. What the (censored) do you mean, what is my opinion of his performance? I mean (censored), that's a tough question to ask me, isn't it?

> **Tommy Lasorda, after the Cubs' Dave Kingman**
> **hit three homers and drove in eight runs**
> **to beat the Dodgers, 1981**

What makes a good pinch-hiter? I wish to hell I knew.

> **Bobby Murcer, former Cubs outfielder**
> *Inside Sports,* 1982

Gravel Gerty [was] the greatest beer vendor in Cub history. Actually, if they had put him in the lineup, he would have hit better than most Cubs.

Mike Royko
Chicago Sun-Times, 1983

I thought I was throwing O.K. So did the hitters, I guess.
Ferguson Jenkins, giving up six runs in the first inning
The Sporting News, 1983

I've never even come close to one before, and I hope I never have to do it again.
Ron Cey, Cubs infielder, on his inside-the-park home run at Wrigley Field, 1983

I don't care how far it went. I just wanted a new ball.
**Dick Ruthven, Cubs pitcher,
on a 425-foot homer to Keith Hernandez, 1984**

I haven't batted in ten years, and they send me out to face Mario Soto.
**Dennis Eckersley, Cubs pitcher,
coming over from the American League, 1984**

I'm going to flash the hitters the home-run sign.
Jim Frey, Cubs manager, 1984

I still can't remember touching all the bases. For all I know, I didn't touch any.
**Brian Dayett, Cubs outfielder, on his pinch-hit,
game-winning grand slam against the Reds, 1985**

I've got a quiet nine-game hitting streak. Don't tell anybody.
Bob Dernier, Cubs centerfielder
Chicago Tribune, 1985

We're paying for the balls, hit 'em!
Don Zimmer, Cubs coach, to the team in batting practice
Chicago Sun-Times, 1985

I know how the kid feels. I had a slump once, too. Except mine lasted twelve years.
Don Zimmer, on Ryne Sandberg's slump
Chicago Tribune, 1985

What about my pride, having to bat a .160 hitter in the cleanup spot?
Jim Frey, Cubs manager, when Ron Cey said not batting fourth hurt his pride, 1985

You see guys these days. They don't even want to *swing* at the ball. No, they run up at it and *slap* at it, trying to hit it into the carpet so it can bounce thirty feet in the air. And the worst part of it is . . . *some of these guys actually get on base!*
Jim Frey
Baseball Digest, 1985

I just ordered some new bats. Can you believe it? They sent me a whole shipment of bats and not one set of instructions.
Steve Lake, Cubs catcher, hitting .152 in July
Chicago Sun-Times, 1985

Hey, I might lose twenty-five pounds and be hitting my weight. No, sorry, I got carried away. I'd still have a long way to go.
Steve Lake, hitting .131 in August
"Cubs Baseball," WGN-TV, Chicago, 1985

I'm a .239 hitter. Things have looked blurry all my life.
> **Don Zimmer, Cubs coach, on getting hit**
> **in the head in spring training, 1986**

The players all love him [manager Jim Frey] dearly and would all volunteer to cut thirty points off their batting averages if it would take the heat off this fine man. . . . Some of them already have given up fifty, even sixty points.
> **Bernie Lincicome**
> *Chicago Tribune*, 1986

Hitters tend to remind you when it was a really bad pitch.
> **Steve Stone, former Cubs pitcher**
> "Cubs Baseball," WGN-TV, Chicago, 1986

26. Fielding and Running

Though the deduction is hardly orthodox, I am sure the Lord helped me catch that ball, and it was my first experience in prayer.
> **Billy Sunday, on when the White Stockings**
> **centerfielder caught a long fly in 1886**

Evers to Tinker to Chance. Those double plays have done much damage to our boys [the Giants] here in Chicago.
> **William F. Kirk**
> *New York American*, 1908

These are the saddest of possible words:
"Tinker to Evers to Chance."
Trio of bear cubs, and fleeter than birds,
Tinker and Evers and Chance.
Ruthlessly pricking our gonfalon bubble,
Making a Giant hit into a double—
Words that are heavy with nothing but trouble:
"Tinker to Evers to Chance."

Franklin P. Adams
New York Globe, 1908

You newspapermen have done very well by Tinker, Evers, and Chance. In fact, you have built up a fake.

John McGraw, Giants manager, 1908

It still seems that McGraw was right; Tinker to Evers to Chance was an overrated combination. They should have taken Franklin P. Adams into the Hall of Fame with them.

Glenn Dickey
The History of National League Baseball, 1979

Don't let anyone tell you the poet's pen isn't mightier than the official scorer's pencil.

Warren Brown, Chicago sportswriter

The spectators take for granted really wonderful catches and unless the outfielder is compelled to climb a tree, turn a double somersault, leap over a ten foot bleacher fence, or do something equally sensational, he scarcely attracts attention.

Johnny Evers
Baseball in the Big Leagues, 1910

You can shake great fielders out of trees but good hitters are hard to come by.

Rogers Hornsby, Cubs manager

There's no such thing as a bad hop. It's the way you played it.
                        Leo Durocher, Cubs manager

He ought to be taken out behind the barn and shot.
                  Leo Durocher, on a poor fielding third baseman

There's nothing tough about playing third. All a guy needs is a strong arm and a strong chest.
                        Frankie Frisch, Cubs manager

I was watching a spider crawl through the ivy. What else was there to do out there in a game like that?
                   José Cardenal, Cubs outfielder,
                   when the Cubs lost, 22–0, to the Pirates, 1975

I won't have any trouble fielding the ball as long as they don't hit it to me.
                   Richie Hebner, future Cub infielder
                   Sports Illustrated, 1982

A guy could get hurt out there.
                   Joe Carter, Cubs outfielder,
                   after the team muffed four flies in two games, 1983

When a baseball goes up in the air, it should be caught. When it isn't, it bothers our pitching staff.
                   Dallas Green, Cubs general manager, 1984

Just give me somebody who can catch the ball. At least once in a while.
                   Jim Frey, Cubs manager,
                   looking for an outfield, 1984

I remember I did that once, and I burned my glove.
Lou Boudreau,
after Larry Bowa made consecutive errors
"Cubs Baseball," WGN-Radio, Chicago, 1985

I know that being active in sports as a youngster gave me a lot of the ability that I have today. Not that catching toads helps me catch balls, but who knows?
Ryne Sandberg
Ryno!, 1985

I've always had one philosophy about defense: You cheat, lie, steal, or do anything you can to get the other guy out.
Jay Johnstone
Temporary Insanity, 1985

Today, I just don't know. I just played with reckless abandon. It's usually not a good idea to be jumping into brick walls.
Davey Lopes, on his two great catches
Chicago Tribune, 1985

After you learn all the angles in this park, you could probably become a good pool player. . . . On any given day, those lovely ivy-covered walls can bring you to your knees.
Keith Moreland, Cubs right fielder
Cubs Vine Line, 1986

We spent the first couple innings as if we were adjusting to a new time zone.
Jim Frey, on a five-error game in San Diego
Chicago Tribune, 1986

You fresh busher. You come into me like that again, and I'll stick this ball down your throat. If you ever cut me, you'll never play another game in the big leagues.

> **Johnny Evers, Cubs second baseman, when rookie
> Casey Stengel slid hard into second base, 1912**

For a while there, I didn't get along very good with Johnny Evers.

> **Casey Stengel**

He runs too long in one place. He's gotta lot of up 'n down, but not much forward.

> **Dizzy Dean, Cubs pitcher, on a slow runner**

When the wind is blowing in, don't try to steal any bases. The wind will stop you.

> **José Cardenal, Cubs outfielder,
> his theory on how to play Wrigley Field**

There's no place for it in the textbook. It's a little like knowing what an intimate friend is going to say a split-second before he says it.

> **Lou Brock, on knowing when to steal
> *Stealing Is My Game*, 1976**

I can't offer a scrap of evidence that black athletes run faster than whites, but every time I look out on a playing field or track, that's what I see.

> **Bill Veeck**

I had a brain spasm.

> **Tim Blackwell, Cubs catcher,
> on why he stopped between first and second base, 1981**

My main problem is getting to first base.

Davey Lopes, Cubs infielder,
when asked if he might steal more, 1984

For the old Cubs, "run" was a word always followed by "into trouble." They ate more shoe leather than they wore out.

Phil Hersh
Chicago Tribune, 1984

Davis: I'm going to steal third base one of these days. You just watch, Skip, I'm going to put the hammer down and hook third.
Frey: Just one word of caution. You'd better make it.

Jody Davis and Jim Frey
The Sporting News, 1985

27. Cub Fans

Our audiences are composed of the best class of people in Chicago, and no theater, church, or place of amusement contains a finer class of people than can be found in our grandstands.

Albert G. Spalding, White Stockings owner, 1883

Chicago presents the spectacle of a great city positively raving over baseball. Everything else is forgotten—politics, business, home, and family.

New York Herald, 1908

Baseball is for the little man.

Philip K. Wrigley, Cubs owner, on fans

They ride us hard but at least they come out and lose with us.
                    Phil Cavarretta, Cubs infielder, 1953

One thing you learn as a Cubs fan: When you bought your
ticket, you could bank on seeing the bottom of the ninth.
                    Joe Garagiola, former Cubs catcher

I say you ought to put a cage over 'em.
                    **Mudcat Grant, Cardinals pitcher,
                    on the Bleacher Bums, 1969**

There is no known cure for "Cub-ism."
                    Bill Berg, WGN-Radio sportscaster, 1971

Wrigley Field fans are extremely loyal, not only when a player
wore the uniform but after we retired. It was like if you played
for the Cubs you were all right in their minds forever.
                    Glenn Beckert, former Cubs second baseman

Cubs fans generally hibernate in the winter. Only those fans
who slip on the ice are reminded of the Cubs.
                    Rick Schwab
                    Stuck on the Cubs, 1977

Cheerleader: Cubbies whooo! Cubbies whooo! Cubbies whooo!
Cubbies whooo!
Melody: You're gonna have throat cancer in two years if you
keep that up.
Cheerleader: Lady, anything for the Cubs.
                    Organic Theatre Company
                    Bleacher Bums, 1977

If you can just play .500 ball for Cub fans they are happy. Can you imagine what they'd be like if you ever won a pennant for them?

Herman Franks, Cubs manager, 1978

Lloyd: The fellows in the bleachers are stripped to the waist and drinking in the sunshine.
Boudreau: And that's not all they're drinking in.

Vince Lloyd and Lou Boudreau
"Cubs Baseball," WGN-Radio, Chicago

Maybe that's what happens when you haven't won a pennant for thirty-five years. If I'd started watching the Cubs as a boy and ended up empty with my grandchildren sitting beside me, I might boo Kingman myself.

Scot Thompson, Cubs outfielder,
on rowdy fans on Dave Kingman T-shirt day, 1980

A Cub fan sees diamonds where others see broken glass.

Steve Daley
Chicago Tribune

New York didn't need that 1969 pennant. . . . All Cub fans wanted was that one measly pennant. It would have kept us happy until the twenty-first century. But New York took it from us, and I can never forgive that.

Mike Royko
Chicago Sun-Times, 1981

Where I'm from, throwing a Cubs hat on the floor is like throwing the American flag on the ground.

Tom Dreesen, when Letterman abused his hat
"Late Night with David Letterman," NBC-TV, 1982

Cub fans have suddenly become gripped by pennant fever. We're the only fans in America who go crazy over a team that has lost 54 percent of its games. . . . In some cities, when a team loses 54 percent of its games, the manager is fired and the stands are empty. Here, the fans begin calling the team "Destiny's Darlings."

Mike Royko
Chicago Sun-Times, 1983

Rip 'em, rip those country suckers like they rip my players. Eighty-five percent of the people in this country work and the other 15 percent come out here and boo my players. It's a playground for them.

Lee Elia, Cubs manager, 1983

Cubs fans don't get old . . . they only get better. And more loyal—if that is possible.

Bob Ibach and Ned Colletti
Cub Fan Mania, 1983

It's been fun to watch the businessmen coming to the park. . . . Three-piece suits and an attaché case. The coat and vest go in the case and out comes the Cubs cap.

Bill Veeck, in the bleachers
Sports Illustrated, 1984

An afternoon at Wrigley Field is the greatest buy in the country. It's sitting in the sun, drinking a few beers and telling a few lies. You can't beat the price or the entertainment.

Bill Veeck, 1984

It's hostile, very hostile in Wrigley Field. At what other stadium do fans yell, "Throw it back," when an opposing player hits a home run in batting practice?

Ron Darling, Mets pitcher, 1984

They [Cubs management] fear that by tossing the ball back on the field, you could injure one of the Cubs outfielders. The way the Cubs outfielders handle fly balls, these fears could be justified.

Mike Royko
Chicago Tribune, 1986

Every time I turn around I run into a Cubs fan. I wonder where they were when I was playing?

Joe Garagiola, former Cubs catcher
"Game of the Week," NBC-TV, 1984

Now that I'm retired as Mets hitting instructor, I'm free to root for the Cubbies.

Phil Cavarretta, former Cub, 1984

Once a Cub, always a Cub.

Ernie Banks, 1984

Eventually, the no-shirt-off-in-the-boxes rule was abolished during one of the team's ninety-loss seasons (apparently because there was no one in the boxes to offend).

Dan Brown
Chicago Magazine, 1984

Cubs fans remember the strangest things.

Mike Royko
Chicago Tribune, 1984

Real Cubs fans are 99.44 percent scar tissue. A fast start by the Cubs causes them no palpitations. Such feints are traditionally followed by faints.

George Will
Newsweek, 1984

George [Will] is a Chicago Cubs fan, a member of that very, very small band of brothers and sisters who year after year took pride in rooting for a team that had been in the cellar so many times the Preservations Society on Monuments had declared it a National Fallout Shelter.

Art Buchwald
Washington Post, 1984

We won a couple, and Cub fans are acting like it's New Year's Eve.

Jim Frey, Cubs manager, 1984

I am supposed to be nonpartisan and on everybody's side, but I was kind of upset there before the television when they didn't go all the way.

Ronald W. Reagan, 1984

Ah, Cubbie fans. Patient and loyal like the family dog. Caring like the family nurse. Forgiving like the family priest. Fans of the Chicago Cubs *are* family. From old ladies to babies, they gather in daylight to cheer till twilight.

Joe Goddard
Bill Mazeroski's Baseball, 1985

He has raised his son to be a Cubs fan. It seems cruel.

William E. Geist
Esquire, 1985

When you're a Cubs fan, you *can* go home again.

Jim Langford, Cubs author
Esquire, 1985

Cubs fans are more interested in the game than jumping up and down yelling, "We're Number One!" People who do that aren't real baseball fans.

Bill Hickman, writer
Esquire, 1985

To be a Cub fan is to worry. It was, before last year in fact, the chief advantage to being one.

Bernie Lincicome
Chicago Tribune, 1985

Cub fans understand this sort of thing better than anyone. They've been one pitch away from something good for quite a while. Somehow that one pitch turns into one inning, one game, one home stand, and—whoops!—it's wait-'til-next-year time again.

Bob Logan
So You Think You're a Die-Hard Cub Fan, 1985

Yes, you gotta have heart. There is no other way to survive in life. To Cub fans it's more than a phrase—it is a set of words to live by.

Ned Colletti
You Gotta Have Heart, 1985

Being a Chicago Cubs fan is like being in limbo, with paradise always a day away.

Bryant Gumbel, television host and Cubs fan
Esquire, 1985

To be a true Cubs fan is to root for the Christians to have a big inning against the lions.

Lyn Nofziger, presidential aide

I read the scripture of Daniel in the lions' den before coming
to the ballpark. I tell you, it's *rough* out there.

Tim Flannery, Padres infielder
Sports Illustrated, 1985

I've had sections yell at me, but never an entire stadium.

Steve Garvey, Padres first baseman
Chicago Tribune, 1985

Chicago's wild, I'll tell you. But it's great to go there because
someone in the stands will say one of those funny lines, and
I'll laugh for five or ten minutes.

Tony Gwynn, Padres outfielder
Chicago Tribune, 1985

They told me to stand up, and to get out of the hole I was
standing in. Then they asked me if I'd gotten separated from
my high school field trip. Finally, they just told me I stink.
Tough crowd.

Len Dykstra, 5-foot 10-inch Mets outfielder
The Sporting News, 1985

In New York they will amaze you with their knowledge of the
game. If you get a runner over to the next base, even though
you make an out, they know when to applaud. Cubs fans loved
you whether you got the guy over or not.

Jay Johnstone
Temporary Insanity, 1985

In Los Angeles, they expect you to win. In Chicago, they hope.

Ron Cey, Cubs infielder, 1985

She was a great fan, saw our games on TV. She'll have a better seat now.

Bob Dernier, Cubs outfielder, on his late grandmother
The Sporting News, 1985

It's funny how you get a lot of letters from fans. At least they care and know you're still breathing. But the remedies seldom work.

Richie Hebner, Cubs infielder
Chicago Tribune, 1985

We drove through the streets [in San Diego] past fans wearing Cubs hats so old and wrinkled that the emblem was twisted. Some of these fans were so old they could barely raise their hands to say good-bye. I just sat on the bus, saying, "Jesus Christ, how long has he been a Cubs fan? I don't know him from Adam. But I don't want to let him down."

Gary Matthews, Cubs outfielder
Sport, 1985

My heart told me to come back to Chicago. After the way things went last year, I guess I became a Cub fan.

Rick Sutcliffe, Cubs pitcher
Time, 1985

But for the fans, there never was anyplace to compare with Wrigley Field. All parks should be like that, and the people there were something special. They came to sit in the sun and watch baseball, not to boo the players.

Frankie Baumholtz, former Cub outfielder
Chicago Tribune, 1986

There's a different perspective at Wrigley Field—a clearer understanding of failure as a consistent part of baseball. Because ball teams play every day, the chances for failure are always high, but the Cubs fans somehow understand that. It's a higher level of baseball culture.

> **Roy Eisenhardt, Oakland A's president**
> *The New Yorker*, 1986

28. Umpires

Q: Can an umpire change his decision?
A: Yes, but not without getting himself disliked.

> ***Spalding's Official Baseball Guide*, 1878**

The average league umpire is a worthless loafer.

> ***Chicago Tribune*, editorial, 1880s**

The chances are our earliest ballplayers learned the game hurling nuts at each other from tops of palm trees. It does not require much of a stretch of the imagination to believe that Abel probably gave a bad decision in favor of the Ham Giants, and that Cain slew him with a bat.

> **Johnny Evers**
> *Baseball in the Big Leagues*, 1910

The slugging of umpires by players is no longer an essential part of the programme, and their mobbing by spectators, though occasionally indulged in, is not encouraged by public opinion.

> **Albert G. Spalding**
> *America's National Game*, 1911

Oh, Hack, if the bat hits the ground, you're out of the game.

> **Beans Reardon, umpire, when Cubs outfielder
> Hack Wilson threw his bat protesting a call**

A manager arguing with an umpire is like arguing with a stump. Maybe you city folks don't know what a stump is. Well, it's something a tree has been cut down off of.

> **Dizzy Dean, Cubs pitcher**

The first man to touch this blind old man is fined fifty bucks.

> **Charlie Grimm, Cubs manager, when his players
> ran out onto the field protesting umpire
> Charlie Moran's call**

I tried every place to get a blue serge suit. But I'm doggoned, they just aren't to be had.

> **Lon Warneke, former Cubs pitcher,
> returning as an umpire, 1949**

You know, Mac, for twenty years as a player I thought that was a ball, too. But it's a strike, so I went to umpiring.

> **Dusty Boggess, umpire, when Cubs catcher
> Clyde McCullough protested a called third strike**

Umpires are just like policemen. A cop could jump in the river to save a child from drowning, and the mother would be liable to ask, "Where's the cap?"

> **Rogers Hornsby**
> *My War with Baseball*, 1962

I made the perfect pitch. It hit the batter, it hit the catcher, then it hit the umpire.

> **Pete Mikkelson, Cubs pitcher**

Magerkurth: I'll reach down and bite your head off.
Durocher: If you do, you'll have more brains in your stomach than you've got in your head.

**Leo Durocher, Cubs manager,
to umpire George Magerkurth**

Froemming: If I called a pitch like that a strike, I wouldn't be able to sleep nights.
Pappas: Then how in the hell do you sleep all those other nights when you blow those calls?

**Milt Pappas, Cubs pitcher, to umpire Bruce Froemming,
when a walk to the last batter cost Pappas a
perfect game, 1972**

It had never happened to me before, and I didn't know what I was supposed to do. So I just went into the clubhouse and sat in my uniform in front of my locker until the game was over. I felt like I was sitting in a corner in school.

Larry Bowa, Cubs infielder, on his first ejection, 1983

If a star like Musial or Williams took a close pitch and the umpire wasn't sure, it was always a ball. But if I took the same pitch, it was a strike. And when I beefed it was, "How would you know—you haven't played since Ash Wednesday!"

Joe Garagiola, former Cubs catcher
Inside Sports, 1983

They [the umpires] were pretty consistent—'course I was only in there 5⅓ innings, so I can only tell you about half the game.

Dennis Eckersley, Cubs pitcher
Chicago Tribune, 1984

I used to bark at umpires, but that was when I was younger. Now, I'm older and calmer. Oh, maybe there's an occasional growl, but that's it.

> **Bill "Mad Dog" Madlock, former Cubs infielder**
> *USA Today*, 1985

I have been called out on some ridiculous calls sometimes, but I have swung at some ridiculous pitches, too.

> **Gary Matthews**
> *They Call Me Sarge*, 1985

29. Utility Players and Trades

I had learned to know the value of good newspaper advertising, and it came good and plenty as long as King Kelly remained to weep and wail over his sad fate in being sold away from the city he loved so well.

> **Albert G. Spalding, White Stockings owner, 1887**

I don't care what kind of bench I got. A carpenter can give me a good bench.

> **Rogers Hornsby, Cubs manager**

We were in New York at the time, at the Commodore Hotel. I remember Larry MacPhail called me on the telephone at about two in the morning. "I've just made a deal for you," he said. "At two in the morning?" I asked. "What's the difference?" he said.

> **Billy Herman, on being acquired**
> **by the Cubs from the Dodgers in 1941**

Sometimes the best deals are the ones you don't make.

Bill Veeck

I was just there—that's it.
Daryl Robertson, Cubs infielder on his nine-game
major-league career with the Cubs in 1962

And then there is the nightmare to end all nightmares—Lou
Brock for Ernie Broglio!
Jim Enright, sportswriter, on the trade which sent Brock,
Jack Spring, and Paul Toth to the Cardinals for
Broglio, Bobby Shantz, and Doug Clemens in 1964

Decker: Brock! This guy's gonna be in the Hall of Fame, and
we traded him for that bum Broglio.
Organic Theatre Company
Bleacher Bums, 1977

Brock for Broglio? P. K. Wrigley is still swallowing his gum
over that one.
Edward Kiersh
Where Have You Gone, Vince DiMaggio?, 1983

Take solace in the knowledge
That, whatever else can be said of you,
You didn't trade Brock for Broglio.
Jim Langford
The Cub Fan's Guide to Life, 1984

Brock cried when he was traded. Cub fans have been crying
ever since.
Ned Colletti
You Gotta Have Heart, 1985

I was amazed to discover the relief staff of the 1980 Chicago
Cubs. How would you like to call on middle relievers Dick
Tidrow, Dennis Lamp, Rick Reuschel, or Mike Krukow and
then call on Bill Caudill, Bruce Sutter or Willie Hernandez to
finish up? I guess that says it all about the Cubs. If you don't
believe me, ask Lou Brock or Ernie Broglio.

Keith R. Stanzel II, letter
The Sporting News, 1985

We confused some people a bit because they couldn't see the
game plan. . . . Every time I made a trade they thought I was
trading Lou Brock again.

Dallas Green, Cubs president
Sport, 1985

The Chicago sportswriters agreed it was a wonderful deal.
The St. Louis scribes knocked it. . . . Brock has since been
elected to the Hall of Fame. Broglio is selling booze in San
Jose, California.

Jerome Holtzman
Chicago Tribune, 1986

I think the Cardinals got the benefit of my maturing at that
point, and the Cubs probably gave up a couple of weeks too
soon.

Lou Brock, 1973

It doesn't bother me any more that I'll always be remembered
as the other guy in the Lou Brock deal. . . . What can I do? I
didn't make the trade.

Ernie Broglio, 1982

If there'd been a team in Outer Mongolia, the Cubs would
have sent me there.

Ferguson Jenkins, on his trade to Texas, 1974

Why couldn't the Cubs have discovered Koufax? I asked Vic. "What would it have mattered?" he said. "They would have traded him before he developed anyway."

> **Barry Gifford**
> *The Neighborhood of Baseball,* 1981

I went from the Pittsburgh Pirates to the Chicago Cubs. You know what that's like? That's like getting the beer concession at a Billy Graham rally.

> **Joe Garagiola**
> "The John Davidson Show," CBS-TV, 1981

Being traded is like celebrating your 100th birthday. It might not be the happiest occasion in the world, but consider the alternatives.

> **Joe Garagiola**

There was nothing glamorous about it. If you cut yourself shaving, the manager would usually give you three or four days off.

> **Joe Garagiola, on being a utility player**

Just so if I ever got down, I'll remember that things aren't as bad as they could be.

> **Bill Caudill, keeping his old Cubs hat in his locker**
> *Sports Illustrated,* 1982

I sent Ernie Banks a telegram, saying, "I left all the base hits in the jersey for you."

> **Paul Schramka, no at-bats in his Cub career,**
> **who played with Ernie Banks' number, 1982**

People ask me where I live, and I tell them, "In escrow."
**Mike Krukow, pitcher, who went from the Cubs to
the Phillies to the Giants in one year, 1984**

I wasn't a good player, but I was always the most popular player. That's like getting the Miss Congeniality award at a beauty contest.
Jim Frey, Cubs manager
Chicago Tribune, 1983

Did it hurt to see the Penguin go? Do you cry at the end of *Lassie*?
Tommy Lasorda, on losing Ron Cey to the Cubs
The Artful Dodger, 1985

Last year the Cubs couldn't beat the Hilton Hotel cooks. A few trades later we're champs.
Richie Hebner, Cubs outfielder, 1984

At least I'm going to the Phils instead of some place like the Mets.
Bill Campbell, pitcher, traded by the Cubs, 1984

The Cubs? Why, they've traded away some of the greatest players in the entire history of baseball.
Jim Belushi, comedian and actor
Esquire, 1985

I remember the day it happened. I called my mom; she cried. I called my sister; she cried. I called my father; he cried. I cried. I was so happy.
Bill Caudill, on his coming to the Cubs from the Reds
Sport, 1985

I was a utility outfielder for the Cubs in 1973. Home opener against Montreal, ninth inning, tie game. I was put in to pinch-run. . . . I'm standing on third base, petrified. If we don't score there, I'm thinking, I've got to go in and play third. . . . With the bases loaded, Marshall walks in the winning run. I wasn't happy. I was ecstatic.

Tony LaRussa
Chicago Tribune, 1986

Caray: Von Hayes has great speed, great bat, good arm. He's developed into a full-fledged star. Whatever happened to the five guys the Indians got for him?
Stone: The Cubs have them now.

Harry Caray and Steve Stone
"Cubs Baseball," WGN-TV, Chicago, 1986

When the Twins and Cubs made their five-player deal involving George Frazier, Ray Fontenot, and Ron Davis, one general manager quipped, "That goes to show that you can trade *anyone* if you try hard enough."

Peter Gammons
Sports Illustrated, 1986

Any team that has ever made a trade with the Cubs is not allowed to laugh in public for at least ten years.

Bernie Lincicome
Chicago Tribune, 1986

I didn't even know they played baseball down there. I thought they still lived in huts. I thought I'd be living in a teepee or something.

**Steve Hamilton, Cubs minor-league pitcher,
playing in Venezuela, 1986**

30. World Series

They still do play a World Series, don't they? It's been so long I don't remember.

Philip K. Wrigley, Cubs owner, 1966

Q: What does a mama bear on the pill have in common with the World Series?
A: No Cubs.

Harry Caray, Cubs broadcaster, 1983

I never thought the Cubs would go so long without a pennant. I thought they'd win one accidentally.

Andy Pafko, former Cubs outfielder, 1984

You never get over not winning it and not going to the World Series. Never.

Billy Connors, Cubs pitching coach, 1984

Does anyone realize that Halley's Comet will have visited us twice since the last time the Cubs won a World Series?

Robert Czak, letter
The Sporting News, 1985

1910: Athletics Defeat Cubs 4 Games to 1

So you're the pups who think you can beat us.

Johnny Evers, Cubs infielder
to underdog opponent Jack Barry, 1910

269

1929: Athletics Defeat Cubs 4 Games to 1

Sometimes I think nine trained monkeys could do better in a Series than the apes we pay salaries.

Joe McCarthy, Cubs manager,
following the Series, 1929

1932: Yankees Defeat Cubs 4 Games to 0

I never pose for any pictures on days when I'm going to pitch. Superstitious, hell! I just think it's unlucky.

Lon Warneke, Cubs pitcher,
before Game Two, 1932

Babe uncoiled one of those beautiful swings. *Crack*! I can still see that ball going out of Wrigley Field. Have you ever seen a golf ball take off? That's the way that ball shot into the air, just like a golf ball. It got so small in such a hurry it looked like it was shrinking as it went.

Joe Sewell, on Ruth's famous called
home run off Charlie Root in Game Three

I was sitting within a few feet of Ruth when he pointed, and it wasn't any myth: he was pointing towards the bleachers. You can forget that indicating-the-count stuff. Ruth called his shot, pure and simple.

Pat Pieper, Cubs public address announcer

I was there and saw and I saw the Babe point toward center-field. The crowd knew it meant one thing—he was going to hit Root's next pitch out of the park. He did, too.

Grantland Rice, sportswriter

He didn't point. If he had, I'd have knocked him on his fanny.
I'd have loosened him up. I took my pitching too seriously to
have anybody facing me do that.

Charlie Root, Cubs pitcher

You undoubtedly think Babe Ruth was pointing to the bleachers for a home run he was about to hit that day in Chicago in
1932. Wrong. The umpire had just asked him where the gent's
room was.

Jim Murray
Los Angeles Times

I've been listening to that bullshit so long. If he'd done that
our pitcher would have had him in the dirt.

Burleigh Grimes, former Cubs pitcher, 1985

1935: Tigers Defeat Cubs 4 Games to 2

What's going on here? It's them same two teams that were
playing each other in Detroit!

Mike Jacobs, boxing czar,
when the Series moved to Chicago, 1935

I have always prided myself on a command of lurid expres-
sions. I must confess that I learned from these young fellows
some variations on the language even I didn't know existed.

Commissioner Landis, on the bench-jockeying

Jolly Cholly Grimm was a big-hearted fellow. He was so gen-
erous he helped give the Detroit Tigers the 1935 World Series
championship. There's nothing wrong with that except that he
was manager of the opposing Chicago Cubs at the time.

Bruce Nash and Allan Zullo
The Baseball Hall of Shame, 1985

1938: Yankees Defeat Cubs 4 Games to 0

Dizzy Dean didn't have anything but a change of pace. First he would throw a slow ball. Then he would throw a slower ball. Then he would throw one so lazy, so soft, so absolutely devoid of stuff, that a handwriting expert sitting in the stands would have read Ford Frick's character from his signature on the ball.

**George Kirksey, sportswriter,
on the Cubs pitcher's poor performance**

1945: Tigers Defeat Cubs 4 Games to 3

I don't think either team is capable of winning.
**Warren Brown, Chicago sportswriter,
on the poor quality of both teams, 1945**

It is the fat men against the tall men at the annual office picnic.
Frank Graham, New York sportswriter, 1945

The worst game of baseball ever played in this country.
Charles Einstein, sportswriter, on Game Six

It was the richest and the poorest World Series ever played.
Warren Brown, on the big crowds and poor play

31. Voices of Cub Fans

Once again you have rewarded your many and long-suffering fans with a patented collapse. Never have I seen such good individual talent jell together to form such a collective failure. Do your fans a favor next spring: when you go to Arizona for spring training . . . stay there.

> **Richard W. Sexton, letter**
> *Chicago Tribune*, 1974

A [Bleacher] Bum told me once why they keep coming to games. "Dem Cubbies need us's encouragement. We encrunge them to dos good. They good dey duz, the betters we feels. Also, the more beers we drinks, the betters we feels."

> **Rick Schwab**
> *Stuck on the Cubs*, 1977

Zig, to his wife: No, I don't want no egg salad sandwich. When you're at the ballgame you don't eat egg salad sandwiches. You eat hot dogs!

> **Organic Theatre Company**
> *Bleacher Bums*, 1977

Greg: And then at the end of the season they're gonna win the pennant. Oh, Marv, could you see that? . . . And they'll play the Series and it'll go the full seven games. And they'll be in the seventh game and it'll be all tied up in the twenty-third inning. . . . And then you know what's gonna happen? They're gonna bring in Ernie Banks out of retirement, and he's gonna hit a home run right into my lap and they win! And that's when you can give me a ride home, Marv.

> **Organic Theatre Company**
> *Bleacher Bums*, 1977

I'm going to be buried in the [Cubs] uniform because baseball is all I think about. It's my life. I don't care about cars or anything else, and never have. . . . They're my life. Without the Cubs I'd be crazy.

Maniford "Hack" Harper, age sixty-five,
Washburn, Illinois, 1980

My dad was in a coma for thirty days in 1980, and when he came out of it, his first words to me were, "We gotta get rid of Kingman."

Jerry Pritikin, advertising executive, 1980

On May 10, 1932, the Chicago Cubs walloped the New York Giants, 9–2. Lon Warneke limited the Giants to five hits, Billy Jurges drove in three runs—and my mother struck out.

Eddie Gold, *Chicago Sun-Times* sportswriter,
on his birth
Inside Sports, 1981

After Audre and I tied the knot, my informants called me from the ballpark and said the Cubs and Dodgers were knotted 2–2 going into extra innings. . . . Everyone thought I was just a nervous bridegroom. I was, because I didn't know the score.

Eddie Gold, on his marriage
Inside Sports, 1981

Let the organ play the National Anthem,
Have six bullpen pitchers to carry my coffin,
Groundskeepers to clear my path.

Steve Goodman
"A Dying Cub Fan's Last Request," 1981

Double your pleasure,
Double your fun,
Sell the Cubs in Eighty-One!
Banner, Wrigley Field, 1981

Cub Fever—Catch It and Die.

Sign, Wrigley Field, 1981

You don't want to know what goes on down there in those box
seats. . . . Heck, we take bets on Opening Day to see when the
Cubs will lose their 100th game.
Barbara Sullivan, West Rogers Park, Illinois, 1983

Charlie, there has got to be a Wrigley Field in heaven. And I
bet they play ball every day. No night games. I don't know if
you or I will get to heaven first, but just in case you do, I'm
sending along sixty cents. I'd like you to leave a ticket for me
at the pickup window. I promise I'll look up God as soon as
the game is over—unless it's a doubleheader.
Wayne Lease, Arlington, Texas,
letter to ailing manager Charlie Grimm, 1983

I am a Cub fan. Why? Self defense. I am the wife, mother,
mother-in-law, grandmother and sister-in-law of Cub fans.
When I met my husband, I should have known better.
Louise M. Johnson
The Scoreboard News, 1984

I flew in from Phoenix on a $289 air fare and I'm staying in a
hotel room for $85 a night, all so I could go watch a $3 baseball
game. Isn't America great!
Kevin Kellogg, Phoenix, Arizona, at the
National League Championship Series, Chicago, 1984

I was happy to do it. What the heck? The refrigerator will only last nineteen or twenty years. The Cubs only win every thirty-nine.

**Len Mattioli, trading a refrigerator and stove
($1,900) for two Cubs playoff tickets, 1984**

I'll Trade My Hubby for a Cubby.

T-Shirt, NLCS, Chicago, 1984

I told my boss I couldn't be at work because I had a fever—Cub fever.

Jay Hefferman, at the NLCS, Chicago, 1984

I've been a Cub fan for a long, long time. I came here to scratch my thirty-nine-year itch.

**Phyliss Liss, Elburn, Illinois,
at the NLCS, San Diego, 1984**

I'd be happy to paint my face dark green and sit in the center-field bleachers if they wanted me to.

Martha Soukup, at the NLCS, San Diego, 1984

My wife wanted to go to Paris and London, but I told her that Paris and London would always be there.

**Randy Lightle, honeymooning at the playoffs
Esquire, 1985**

When my grandfather died, he wanted to be frozen and brought out when the Cubs made the playoffs. When they did, my grandmother went to the bleachers and was asked if she brought him. "Yeah," she said, "but I used him to ice the beer."

Tom Dreesen, comedian, 1985

I was asked by *Playgirl* to pose nude, but I would only if I could pose with a Cubs hat over my private parts. They refused, and I said, "That's okay. They don't make Cubs hats that big, anyway."

Tom Dreesen, 1985

The worst thing that happened was that someone stole my Cubs hat.

George Lazansky, Beirut terrorist hostage, 1985

He [Sutcliffe] stinks anyway. Eckersley's the best. Eckersley and Trout can carry 'em. Trust me.

Jim Schultz, age thirteen
Chicago Sun-Times, 1985

It seems he [Dallas Green] has a bad habit of getting rid of good players for lousy pitchers. Will someone please tell me how we can get rid of Dallas Green?

Shirley Hall, Cub fan, on the Davey Lopes trade
Chicago Tribune, 1986

In 1983, the other guys on the Tour were laughing at me. In 1984, they were accusing me of jumping on the bandwagon. In 1985, they were laughing at me again. This year, they don't even want to talk to me.

David Ogrin, professional golfer and Cub fan
Chicago Tribune, 1986

In regard to the 1986 Chicago Cubs, never in the history of major league baseball did so many who were paid so much accomplish so little.

William E. Carsley, letter
The Sporting News, 1986

32. Famous Last Words

Why, Spalding, the wit of man cannot devise a plan or frame a form of government that will control the game of baseball for over five years.

**William A. Hulbert, before he and Albert G. Spalding
formed the Chicago club and the National League, 1875**

If the players league lasts there will be twenty-five cent baseball, Sunday games, beer will flow in the grandstands, and the industry will be ruined by utter destruction.

Albert G. Spalding, White Stockings owner, 1890

The champions [Cubs] still have a chance, but it is thinner than the ham sandwiches at the Philadelphia ball park. Only those who have inhaled said sandwiches know how thin that is.

Charles Dryden, before the Cubs won the pennant
Chicago Tribune, 1908

The real Cub fans are on the West Side. Moving the team's base to the North Shore is a bad idea.

**Charles Murphy, former Cubs president,
on the move to Weeghman Park,
later called Wrigley Field, 1916**

Why, that guy's got a million-dollar arm and a five-cent head. He has no judgment. No instinct. He'll never make a catcher.

**Dan Sullivan, high school baseball coach,
on Gabby Hartnett, future Hall of Famer, 1919**

Jurges: Come down to my room, I've got something for you.
Valli: If you have anything to tell me, come up to my room.
**Violet "I Did It For Love" Valli; before she shot
and seriously wounded Cub shortstop Billy Jurges, 1932**

Just a fad, a passing fancy.
**Philip K. Wrigley, Cubs owner,
on the advent of night baseball, 1935**

I had never seen him hit a long ball and I wanted to challenge him.
**Guy Bush, Cubs pitcher,
on throwing numbers 713 and 714 to Babe Ruth, 1935**

Ballplayers on the road live together. It won't work.
**Rogers Hornsby, former Cubs player/manager,
on the signing of Jackie Robinson, 1945**

The Cubs will come back for more. They have always come back. They always will.
Warren Brown, Chicago sportswriter, 1946

For two years, you have been bothering me, and now you're going to die.
**Ruth Ann Steinhagen, before she shot and wounded
former Cub Eddie Waitkus, and was sent to a
mental institution, 1947**

The 1948 Cubs were the best team ever to finish last in the National League.
Jim Gallagher, Cubs general manager

We needed a roommate for [Gene] Baker.

> **Wid Matthews, Cubs general manager,**
> **on why he brought up Ernie Banks, 1953**

We seem to have been going backwards for the last few years.

> **Philip K. Wrigley, Cubs owner, 1953**

Harry Chiti is the new Gabby Hartnett.

> **Wid Matthews, Cubs general manager, on the**
> **catcher who played 229 games for the Cubs, 1955**

By just analyzing our team on paper, I say it is possible for us to take all the marbles.

> **Robert Whitlow, Cubs athletic director,**
> **on the team that finished ninth, 1962**

I believe the deal puts us in a much better position to make a run for the flag. I think this is going to make us a little more respected.

> **Bob Kennedy, Cubs manager, on the**
> **Lou Brock for Ernie Broglio deal, 1964**

The next day, I wrote a story saying that the Cubs had made a trade that might win them the pennant.

> **Brent Musburger, former Chicago sportswriter,**
> **on the Brock for Broglio trade, 1985**

The Cubs will come alive in '65.

> **Ernie Banks, Cubs shortstop,**
> **on the team that finished eighth, 1965**

It took the White Sox forty years to win their last pennant. At that rate, we've still got twenty years to go.

Philip K. Wrigley, Cubs owner, 1965

He won't make it.

**Gordon Goldsberry, Cubs scout,
on pitcher Tom Seaver, c. 1966**

He took me out of the rotation. That had to bother me. It was an embarrassment. Afterwards, I had some choice words for him on the bench. I told him to get fucked.

**Ernie Broglio, to Cubs manager Leo Durocher,
two days before he was shipped to the minors in 1966**

The Cubs will shoot from the hip with Leo the Lip.

Ernie Banks, Cubs shortstop, 1966

The Cubs aren't an eighth-place club and I'm here to find out why they are where they are.

Leo Durocher, Cubs manager, 1966

I was right, too. It wasn't an eighth-place club. It was a tenth-place club!

Leo Durocher, 1966

The Cubs will be fine in sixty-nine.

Ernie Banks, 1969

I have found the next Willie Mays. What a ballplayer this kid is going to be.

**Leo Durocher, Cubs manager, on outfielder
Oscar Gamble, who played twenty-four
games for the Cubs, 1969**

The "Dump Durocher" clique might as well give up.
Philip K. Wrigley, Cubs owner,
the year before the manager was fired, 1971

When Sutter is ready for the big leagues, that will be the day
the Communists take over.
Walt Dixon, Cubs minor league manager,
reporting on injured pitcher Bruce Sutter, 1972

You think I'm going to miss Chicago! No way! As far as Chicago fans are concerned, the two times we go there to play the
White Sox will be plenty enough for me. . . . I hate this ballpark. It stinks. I never want to pitch here again or anywhere
to the Cubs.

Ken Holtzman, who returned
to the Cubs six years later, 1972

All we need is lightning to strike again like it did in 1935 when
we won twenty games in a row, and the pennant.
Philip K. Wrigley, Cubs owner, 1973

I have outlived my usefulness. Everything has changed.
Philip K. Wrigley, shortly before he died, 1977

My epitaph is inescapable. It will read: "He sent a midget up
to bat."

Bill Veeck, 1976

Veeck, who brought the exploding scoreboard, midgets, clowns
and ethnic nights to baseball, died at the Illinois Masonic
Medical Center of a heart attack.

Associated Press, 1986

Veeck was perhaps best known for sending a midget to the plate.

United Press International, 1986

Look for me under the arc-lights, boys. I'll be back.

Bill Veeck, last lines
Veeck as in Wreck, 1962

I have a question for you guys. Do you think I'm crazy for taking this job?

Herman Franks, Cubs manager, to the media, 1980

We're just backing up so we can get a running start.

Ernie Banks, former Cubs shortstop,
as the Cubs were 11½ games back in May, 1981

He's got the reflexes and hands, but I wonder about his arm. It's okay, but probably not accurate enough for major-league third base. So you might project him in left field or centerfield, where you could take advantage of his speed.

Ed Katalinas, Tigers scout, on the
arm of future Cubs shortstop Shawon Dunston, 1981

I know in my heart the Cubs can't win in daytime baseball.

Dallas Green, Cubs general manager, 1981

It was a mild summer.

Dallas Green, on why the Cubs
won the National League East, 1984

I don't see how I can fail in Chicago.

Bump Wills, Cubs second baseman,
released after one year, 1982

Well, Milo, here we are finishing our first year. A lot of people said we couldn't do it.

> **Harry Caray, to fellow Cubs broadcaster**
> **Milo Hamilton, who was gone by the next year, 1982**

If we could have stayed away from the thirteen-game and eight-game losing streaks, there's no telling what we could have accomplished.

> **Lee Elia, Cubs manager, 1982**

Fuck those fuckin' fans who come out here and say they're Cub fans that are supposed to be behind you, rippin' every fuckin' thing that you do. I'll tell you one fuckin' thing. I hope we get fuckin' hotter than shit, just to stuff it up them 3,000 fuckin' people that show up every fuckin' day, because if they're the real Chicago fuckin' fans, they can kiss my fuckin' ass right downtown and *print it.*

> **Lee Elia, who didn't last the season, 1983**

Looks like he [Randy Martz] is going to mess up the Cubs record of wasting every first-round draft pick. I think he's already the best player they've ever gotten with a number-one pick.

> **Bill James, on the pitcher who didn't last the year**
> *The Bill James Baseball Abstract,* 1983

He still hits enough against lefthanders to help somebody as a platoon player, maybe left fielder or DH. But as a regular, he is through.

> **Bill James, on Davey Lopes**
> *The Bill James Baseball Abstract,* 1983

Who is this Bobby Dernier? He's not going to come in here and take my job. As far as taking my job, well . . . Bobby Dernier doesn't qualify, gentlemen.
**Mel Hall, Cubs centerfielder, before being
traded to the Indians for Rick Sutcliffe, 1984**

Who is Rick Sutcliffe? I hope I face him sometime.
**Mel Hall, Indians centerfielder,
on the pitcher who went 16–1 for the Cubs, 1984**

If the Cubs want to win, I think they should go with me and cut the BS.
**Bill Buckner, Cubs first baseman, before
he went to the Red Sox, who finished fourth, 1984**

The Cubs could go as high as fourth if the Cardinals continue to falter. The bench, though, is weak.
Nick Peters, *Oakland Tribune* sportswriter, 1984

Fifth place. Cubs. New jockey might help. 50–1.
***The Complete Handbook of Baseball*, 1984**

If anybody offers you 100 to 1 odds against Chicago winning the National League East in 1984, take him up on it. . . . If I have ever seen a dead giveaway setup for a miracle, this is it.
**Bill James
The Bill James Baseball Abstract, 1984**

There will be paranoia in the clubhouse and lots of fights. They'll start slowly, then make their move on August 18th and be totally awesome.
Robert Marks, San Francisco astrologer, 1984

The team was the Chicago Cubs. They had two fights during spring training—among themselves. The only "experts" to predict they would win their division were an astrologer from San Francisco and broadcaster Harry Caray.

Fred Mitchell
Chicago Tribune, 1984

They're not that good. Anybody who says they are doesn't know baseball.

Walt Terrell, Mets pitcher, after the Cubs swept four games from the Mets in August, 1984

If a guy's a good pitcher, he's going to play good anywhere. We can play in Istanbul.

Larry Bowa, Cubs infielder,
before the Padres swept the Cubs in San Diego, 1984

You better enjoy this while you can, because the Cubs are the next Milwaukee Brewers.

A National League East club executive, quoted by
Dan McGrath
San Francisco Chronicle, 1984

A lot of managers say they were hired to be fired. Not me. I'm approaching managing as if I'm good enough to be there a while.

Jim Frey, Cubs manager,
fired just over a year later, 1984

Ginny and I join Mrs. George Bush, former Detroit Tigers stars George Kell and Al Kaline, and Vice President George Bush as Kell throws out the first ball of a World Series game between Detroit and the Chicago Cubs, 1984.

Peter Ueberroth, caption in his book
Made in America, 1985

I want to be a star, but if I'm not ready, I don't want to embarrass myself in front of 50,000 people. I'd want to go back now and keep playing. I'd go happy and smiling. But if I do start and they send me back in mid-May, that would be disappointing.

**Shawon Dunston, Cubs shortstop, in March;
in mid-May he was back in Triple-A, 1985**

With Rick Sutcliffe and fellow righthander Dennis Eckersley, add left-hander Steve Trout and righthanders Scott Sanderson and Dick Ruthven, and you have the deepest, healthiest starting rotation in the league. . . . This club will frolic to the division title and a three-game knockout of the Padres.

**Bill Conlin, before the Cubs finished fourth,
23½ games out**
The Sporting News, 1985

They are easily good enough to make it a season-long race with the Mets, but because of that fragile foundation and the burden of history, they'll probably come up just short.

Peter Pascarelli
Sport, 1985

There's no reason Chicago can't make it two in a row.
Nick Peters, *Oakland Tribune* sportswriter, 1985

I'm starting to get chills of excitement already. I get this strange feeling that someone, somewhere already knows how this season is going to end up for us, and we're just going out there to play out the script. I've got a good feeling about this season.

Thad Bosley, Cubs outfielder
Chicago Tribune, 1985

With the pitching performances like we've been getting this season, it already makes me look like a genius.

Jim Frey, Cubs manager, in April
Chicago Tribune, 1985

We could win one hundred games.

Jim Frey, in May
Sports Illustrated, 1985

Geez, the guy [Jim Frey] won a damned championship for this city for the first time since 1945 and six months later they want to fire him? That's not only ridiculous, it's asinine.

Dallas Green, after the Cubs dropped twelve straight in June
Chicago Sun-Times, 1985

Can I have my pick back? You know, the Royals to win the World Series in six games. Big black type on the back page of the paper. . . . As things stand now, my precious Royals have about as much chance of winning the World Series as the Toledo Mud Hens do.

Ron Rapoport, before the Royals won in seven
Chicago Sun-Times, 1985

Injury-free he [Rick Sutcliffe] is one of the best pitchers in baseball. Twenty wins again.

Steve Hanks, on the pitcher who won five and lost fourteen
Sport, 1986

I told him [manager Jim Frey] to forget all the baloney that's been going around and win some games. It's ridiculous talk. It just amazes me that people want to start firing the minute you have a rough go.

> **Dallas Green, on his meeting with Frey in May**
> *The Sporting News*, 1986

If I don't get this team back up there right away, I'll probably be gone by the middle of June.

> **Jim Frey, in April, fired June 13**
> *Chicago Tribune*, 1986

There is no embarrassment on my part. It was very tastefully done.

> **Marla Collins, Cubs ballgirl, on her nude *Playboy* pictorial, before she was fired by the Cubs, 1986**

We're close to being a pretty decent ballclub.

> **Gene Michael, Cubs manager**
> *Chicago Tribune*, 1986

Cubs Selected Bibliography

Ahrens, Art, ed. *The Cubs: The Complete Record of Chicago Cubs Baseball.* New York: Macmillan, 1986.

Over two-thirds of this is taken straight from the *Baseball Encyclopedia,* and much of the rest is a distillation of the same text. There is, however, a short year-by-year Cub history, more roster detail, and team records, and the book is reasonably priced.

Ahrens, Art, and Eddie Gold. *Day by Day in Chicago Cubs History.* Edited by Buck Peden. West Point, N.Y.: Leisure Press, 1982.

This is more than a day-by-day history; it is an excellent record and reference book. It could use a bit more depth, such as biographical information on the owners, coaches, executives, and broadcasters.

Anson, Adrian C. *A Ball Player's Career.* Chicago: Era, 1900.

Ardizzone, Tony. *Heart of the Order.* New York: Henry Holt, 1986.

A novel about growing up on the North Side and into the world of professional baseball. As our hero says, "Every inning I ever played, from the alley in Chicago to Triple-A, was still baseball. Any *real* fan understands that." Sure enough.

Banks, Ernie, and Jim Enright. *Mr. Cub.* Chicago: Follett, 1971.

Banks describes his rough road leading to Cub stardom and idolatry, from life in the South, to the Negro leagues, to a stint in the segregated military. His optimism and genuine love of people in spite of such hardships is very inspiring.

Bartlett, Arthur Charles. *Baseball and Mr. Spalding.* New York: Farrar, Straus, 1951.

An interesting, but rather dry in a 1950s way, account of Spalding's meteoric rise in baseball to his losing campaign for the Senate from California.

Brickhouse, Jack, with Jack Rosenberg and Ned Colletti. *Thanks for Listening.* South Bend, Ind.: Diamond Communications, 1986.

Poorly conceived, badly written, and lacking in candor, this book is hardly a tribute to Mr. Brickhouse's distinguished career. More a barroom chat than a book.

Brock, Lou, and Franz Schulze, *Stealing Is My Game*. Englewood Cliffs, N.J.: Prentice-Hall, 1976.

Although Brock gets top billing, this book is written as a biography by Schulze. Cub fans will find just one chapter, about ten pages, called "Success in the Minors. Then Chicago," on his three years with the team, obviously not the high point of his career.

Brosnan, Jim. *Ron Santo, 3B*. New York: G. P. Putnam's Sons, 1974.

Brosnan, a pitcher with the Cubs for four seasons, is the author of two classics of baseball literature, *The Long Season* and *Pennant Race*. This book is generally aimed at teenagers but displays the same fine reporting and writing.

Caray, Harry, with David Israel. *Holy Cow!* New York: Random House, 1987.

Colletti, Ned. *You Gotta Have Heart*. South Bend, Ind.: Diamond Communications, 1985.

Mr. Colletti's book covers the Dallas Green years, from 1981 to the present. In retrospect, it is interesting to recall how poor and disorganized the team was until the early part of 1984, when the team finally came together. It's nice to read a book about the Cubs with such a happy ending.

Durocher, Leo, with Ed Linn. *Nice Guys Finish Last*. New York: Simon and Schuster, 1975.

Mr. Durocher wasn't loved in Chicago, in baseball, or much in the outside world. Here he is just as acerbic and blunt, especially about some of the Cub players he managed. Nevertheless, despite its self-serving quality, this book is full of baseball lore and is definitely worth reading. Durocher was certainly at the center of things.

Enright, Jim. *Chicago Cubs*. New York: Macmillan, 1975.

Not a detailed and comprehensive history of the team, but if one is looking to discover the story of the oldest franchise in the National League, it is a good place to begin.

Evers, Johnnie, with Hugh S. Fullerton. *Baseball in the Big Leagues*. Chicago: Reilly & Britton, 1910.

Evers describes in detail the thinking man's elements of baseball, a baseball primer, really. Those who don't follow the game religiously will find the book enlightening while those who have already studied the positioning of fielders, for example, might find it tedious.

Farrell, James T. *My Baseball Diary*. New York: A. S. Barnes, 1957.

Although a born White Sox fan, Farrell writes eloquently on growing up in Chicago and on the Cubs. Included are excerpts from his novels, short stories, and reminiscences. A little dry, unless you are a fan of Farrell's naturalistic style.

Fleming, G. H. *The Unforgettable Season*. New York: Holt, Rinehart and Winston, 1981.

Told entirely through press reports, this is the story of the incredible 1908 pennant race among the Cubs, Pirates, and Giants, the year one play by Fred Merkle cost a team a pennant. An unforgettable book, and a must for Cub fans, who can relive the greatest pennant race of all.

Garagiola, Joe. *Baseball Is a Funny Game*. New York: J. B. Lippincott, 1960.

A baseball classic, and still funny after all these years, this book has remained in print now for nearly three decades. Garagiola belonged on the Cubs, and this book belongs on every bookshelf.

Gifford, Barry. *The Neighborhood of Baseball*. New York: E. P. Dutton, 1981. Revised and expanded edition. San Francisco: Creative Arts, 1985.

Gifford is a fine writer: a poet, novelist, and biographer of Jack Kerouac and William Saroyan. His style reminds one of fellow Chicagoan James T. Farrell, and he has fielded a poignant memoir of growing up as he saw it from the Friendly Confines.

Gold, Eddie, and Art Ahrens. *The Golden Era Cubs: 1876–1940*. Chicago: Bonus Books, 1985, and *The New Era Cubs: 1941–1985*. Chicago: Bonus Books, 1985.

Two books that must belong on every Cub fan's bookshelves. Each tells the story of the Cubs through biographical sketches of the players, some of whom were only minor footnotes to Cub history. Funny and informative.

Grimm, Charlie, with Ed Prell. *Jolly Cholly's Story*. Chicago: Henry Regnery, 1968. Republished as *Grimm's Baseball Tales*. Notre Dame, Ind.: Diamond Communications, 1983.

Grimm managed the Cubs for fourteen years, including pennants in three of those years. He was a good-natured guy, and this is a lighthearted book, a pleasant romp through the glory years, especially with the 1935 Cubs, the team he considers his best.

Higbe, Kirby, with Martin Quigley. *The High Hard One.* New York: Viking, 1967.

Higbe broke in with the Cubs, and later spent some glorious years with the Dodgers. Unfortunately, those days of high style ended with his writing this book from jail, but his forthrightness is nice, and he has some strange and hilarious tales to tell.

Hornsby, Rogers. *My Kind of Baseball.* Edited by J. Roy Stockton. New York: David McKay, 1953.

Hornsby describes baseball his way, the "inside game" of stealing, bunting, and sacrificing. He always was a team man, but a nasty coot. As he says, "I'm not known anywhere as 'beloved,' or 'the grand old man of baseball.'" But he could play, and I sure would have liked to see him.

Hornsby, Rogers, and Bill Surface. *My War with Baseball.* New York: Coward-McCann, 1962.

A very good book, as straightforward as any written before the last decade. When Hornsby was managing for Bill Veeck in 1952 and Veeck brought some midgets to spring training, Hornsby tells how he dealt with one: "I picked him up by the seat of the pants and collar and threw him over the railing." Tough guy.

Ibach, Bob, and Ned Colletti. *Cub Fan Mania.* New York: Leisure Press, 1983.

A short tome for Cub fans only by two nice guys from the Cubs publications department. The photography, by Stephen Green, of the fans, the neighborhood, and Wrigley Field, warms your heart and helps you count down the days until spring.

Jenkins, Ferguson, with George Vass. *Like Nobody Else.* Chicago: Henry Regnery, 1973.

Growing up poor, Jenkins learned baseball tossing rocks. He certainly developed a good arm, claiming not only that he could hit any part of a passing train car, but throw it between the boxcar doors if he wanted. I believe him.

Johnstone, Jay, with Rick Talley. *Temporary Insanity.* Chicago: Contemporary Books, 1985.

A rollicking good book, definitely in the top twenty of books on the game. Johnstone prints in full manager Lee Elia's 1983 four-letter tirade, and it was this passage which caused the book to be banned for sale at Dodger Stadium. Johnstone is a Cubbie treasure.

Kinsella, W. P. *The Iowa Baseball Confederacy*. Boston: Houghton Mifflin, 1986.

Baseball fiction is an acquired taste, especially fantasy fiction, but this book is especially powerful. In this lyrical novel, the Cubbies play the Iowa club for 2,614 innings over forty days and forty nights. The reader will hold on until the bitter end.

Langford, Jim. *The Cub Fan's Guide to Life*. Notre Dame, Ind.: Diamond Communications, 1984.

A cute, funny book perfect for entertaining yourself during a rain delay. When my car was stolen and later recovered, everything inside was gone except this book. I still don't know how to take that. The thieves probably got their laughs.

Langford, Jim. *The Game Is Never Over*. South Bend, Ind.: Icarus Press, 1980.

Mr. Langford is an historian and a Cub fan—what a perfect life. His book is a yearly history from 1948 to 1980; it not only reflects his meticulous research but is written to keep any baseball fan enthralled. This book deserves to remain in print. Some historians can write.

Lewine, Peter. *A. G. Spalding and the Rise of Baseball*. New York: Oxford University Press, 1985.

Another baseball book by a professional historian, part of a trend. Why don't these guys teach and leave baseball to the rest of us? Still, an interesting book on the founder of the Cubs, but not as fascinating as Spalding's own autobiography.

Logan, Bob. *Cubs Win!*. Chicago: Contemporary Books, 1984.

A quickie book designed to capitalize on the Cubs success. The pictures and the text could be better, but the book did get out by Christmas and give us something to smile over through that bitter winter.

Logan, Bob. *So You Think You're a Die-Hard Cub Fan*. Chicago: Contemporary Books, 1985.

A nice potpourri of Cub lore, trivia, records, anecdotes, and humorous comments. The text is breezy and informative, a nice book to enjoy on the patio on a sultry evening. Mr. Logan is a veteran *Tribune* sportswriter and knows his stuff. The photographs are memorable!

Marran, David. *The Cub Fan's Quiz Book.* South Bend, Ind.: Diamond Communications, 1985.

If you have a good memory, trivia books are great; I can't remember who won the World Series last year. I know it wasn't the Cubs. The questions in the book are well thought out, and considering that the author is only twenty-one years old, any editor out scouting should consider this kid a prospect.

Matthews, Gary, with Fred Mitchell. *They Call Me Sarge.* Chicago: Bonus Books, 1985.

Although slight, this is a very honest and inspirational book, a real surprise. Matthews details the death of his father, the collapse of his two marriages, and concludes, "You can't be beaten down by disappointments and unfortunate circumstances." A nice gift for a young man going through tough times, such as trying to hit the curve.

Murphy, James M. *The Gabby Hartnett Story.* Smithtown, N.Y.: Exposition Press, 1983.

Mr. Murphy, a Rhode Island newspaperman, was a longtime family friend of Cubs catcher Leo Hartnett. He has written both a warm personal memoir and a well-researched, albeit short, biography. The writing is lively, and the abundant family photographs of the Hartnett clan are worth the price of admission.

Organic Theatre Company. *Bleacher Bums.* New York: Samuel French, 1977. Revised edition: 1980.

A hard-to-find play which you'll either have to get at the library or by ordering from Samuel French. Poignant, with an interesting cast of characters, the ending is bittersweet, as are most Cub seasons. Sometimes shown on public television.

Pepitone, Joe, with Berry Stainback. *Joe, You Coulda Made Us Proud.* Chicago: Playboy Press, 1975.

This book made my hair stand on end, the ultimate in the celebrity self-revealing books of the period. Pepitone describes himself as a lout, liar, loser, and skirt chaser. The man is bad news. Not recommended for heart patients.

Pomeranz, Gary. *Out at Home.* Boston: Houghton Mifflin, 1985.

A novel set in Chicago. Pomeranz offers an explanation of why the Cubs were so lousy: the influence of gambling. A bizarre cast of characters conspires to throw the pennant in 1955. The mystery of whether they throw it or not will not be revealed here, but I will say the ending will be familiar to die-hard Cub fans.

Sandberg, Ryne, with Fred Mitchell. *Ryno!*. Chicago: Contemporary Books, 1985.

I used to love such books when I was a boy. Lots of pictures, big print, and simple text describing our hero. Adults can read it in a half hour and then give it as a gift. A great book to get kids into reading.

Schwab, Rick. *Stuck on the Cubs*. Evanston, Ill.: Sassafras Press, 1977.

An opinionated tome by a dedicated Cub fan, Schwab, an insurance man, offers his views of the Cubs, Wrigley Field, the announcers, and the fans. A nice part is what he describes as "A Cubbie Breakdown," wherein the long-suffering fan finally sees one too many balls slip through fielders' legs and has his annual crack-up. Very funny, but hard to find.

Smith, Curt. *America's Dizzy Dean*. St. Louis, Mo.: Bethany Press, 1978.

Dean, who pitched for the Cubs in his twilight years, should be the subject of a lot more books, the last honest man in America. When he was broadcasting during World War II and couldn't reveal the weather, he said, "I can't tell you folks why this here game is stopped but I'll tell you what. If you just stick your head outside the nearest window, you'll know what I mean."

Spalding, Albert G. *America's National Game*. New York: National Sports Publishing Co., 1911.

A beautiful book to look at, if you can find the original edition at the library. Publishers gave it their all back then. Spalding, a Cubs founder, deserves a monument at Wrigley Field. His book is an important source for anyone interested in the beginnings of the national game. It's a treasure-chest of detail.

Spalding, Harriet I. *Reminiscences of Harriet I. Spalding*. East Orange, N.J., 1910.

Veeck, Bill, with Ed Linn. *The Hustler's Handbook*. New York: G. P. Putnam's Sons, 1965.

A strangely written book. Veeck begins with the art of promotion and then talks rather disparagingly of his fellow owners and executives. This is the man who gave us exploding scoreboards and not a lot of pennants, but who gave us the Wrigley vines, service to the Cubs, and a contribution to baseball which assures his spot in the Hall of Fame.

Veeck, Bill, with Ed Linn. *Veeck—As in Wreck*. New York: G. P. Putnam's Sons, 1962.

Now that Mr. Veeck has passed away, this rather large book remains as part of his legacy. And it's a good one, a great way to revisit the glory days, when owners were baseball men, and ballplayers lived the game. He describes his installation of the scoreboard and the planting of ivy at Wrigley Field and details his futile attempt to have Mr. Wrigley install lights.

Williams, Billy, with Irv Haag. *Billy: The Classic Hitter*. Chicago: Rand McNally, 1974.

Williams' story closely parallels that of Ernie Banks; if Banks hadn't arrived earlier, Billy Williams might have been Mr. Cub. Even Leo Durocher loved him, no mean feat. Instead of publishing books by one-season wonders (especially Mets) this book should be updated and reprinted.

FAN CLUBS

Die-Hard Cub Fan Club, P.O. Box 522, Prospect Heights, Illinois 60070. $9.00.

Membership includes a plastic card, a personalized certificate, two decals, a nice pewter pin, a newsletter, and a copy of the program, the last two of which I've never received. In addition, ticket discounts and an invitation to the national convention are offered. Membership a must.

Die-Hard Cub Fans of Greater Los Angeles, c/o Scott Rosenwald, 1535 Amherst, #205, Los Angeles, California 90025.

Formed in the Fall of 1984 by Cary Kozlow, this club is a cozy neighborhood for displaced Cub fans. Membership totals over 200 and growing.

The Emil Verban Memorial Society, c/o Bruce Ladd, Motorola, 1776 K Street NW, Suite 200, Washington, D.C. 20006. No Dues.

This is the most prestigious of fan clubs. Members must be Cub fans who live in Washington, and the list includes over 400 members such as Ronald Reagan, Bowie Kuhn, Harry Blackmun, David Broder, George Will, Ray Floyd, and Dallas Green. Formed in 1975, the club honors the purely average Cubs infielder with lunches and an occasional newsletter. No dues, no meetings, no officers; as Mr.

Ladd says, "That's why everybody wants in!" They turned me down
—it must be a good club.

Iowa Cubs Fan Club, 916 8th Street, West Des Moines, Iowa
50265. $4.00/year.

Includes the standard identification card, certificate, bumper
sticker, decal and button, and when you throw in a discount on
grandstand seats for three nights, this is quite a deal. Especially
considering that the Triple-A team usually does better than the
parent.

PERIODICALS

The Chicago Baseball Report, P.O. Box 46074, Chicago, Illinois
60646. Monthly. $19.95 ($17.95 to Society of Baseball Research
Members). Editor: John Dewan.

Statistics on the Cubs and White Sox fill this newsletter. It's a
good way to keep up during the season on the numbers you usually
see at year's end, such as slugging percentages, fielding averages,
left/right hitting, and clutch base hits. Essays on the team liven up
the publication.

Cubs Vine Line, P.O. Box 592, Prospect Heights, Illinois 60070.
Monthly. $13.95 ($11.95 to Die-Hard Cub Fan Club members).
Editor: Bob Ibach.

Although begun only in March 1986, this is one of the better
official ballclub monthlies, reflecting the irreverence and knowledge
of editor Bob Ibach and writers such as Eddie Gold, Rick Talley,
and Randy Minkoff. Design is nice also, although the magazine
could do without columns by ballplayers and the manager.

The Minneapolis Review of Baseball, 1501 Fourth Street, Minneapolis, Minnesota 55454. Quarterly. $7.00. Editor: Steve Lehman.

Even though it is based in a nearby state, you'll find a lot of
Chicago baseball here. A recent issue contained a tribute to Bill
Veeck, a profile of Burleigh Grimes, and a clever diary of Chicago
baseball by Judy Aronson. Well worth the money, now in its
seventh year.

The Scoreboard News, P.O. Box 546, Galesburg, Illinois 61401.
Monthly. $14.95. Editor: Jerry D. Johnson.

Begun in the spring of 1985, this attractive publication is basically
a personal newsletter. Although short, usually twelve pages, the
paper is full of insights and revealing statistics. Reports and
articles are always current.

Index

Bob Chieger is a free-lance writer and editor who has been called "the Bartlett of his generation." He has worked for several magazines and publishers, never letting work interfere with baseball. He lives in Portland, Oregon, where he works as a reporter for a local newspaper and an editor for a publishing house. The author of *Voices of Baseball* and three other books, he is single with two season tickets.